"...Not all those who wander are lost."
—J.R.R.Tolkien

Tiny Homes
on the Move
Wheels and Water

Lloyd Kahn

Distributed in the United States by Publishers Group West and in Canada by Publishers Group Canada

Library of Congress Cataloging-in-Publication Data

Kahn, Lloyd, 1935-
  Tiny homes on the move : wheels and water / Lloyd Kahn.
   pages cm
   Includes bibliographical references.
  ISBN 978-0-936070-62-9 (paperback)
  1. Small houses.   2. Mobile home living.   3. Boat living.   I. Title.
  NA7533.K35 2014
  728.7'9—dc23
                             2014001679

5 4 3 2 1 — 16 15 14
(Lowest digits indicate number and year of latest printing.)

Printed and bound in Hong Kong

Shelter Publications, Inc.
P.O. Box 279
Bolinas, California 94924
415-868-0280

Email: shelter@shelterpub.com
Orders, toll-free: 1-800-307-0131

Shelter's Website: www.ShelterPub.com
The Shelter Blog: www.TheShelterBlog.com
Lloyd's Blog: www.LloydKahn.com

Shelter
Publications

Photo on previous page by Mike Basich
Photo at right, Halong Bay, Vietnam, by Hugo Hunt

Vans

Pickup Trucks with Camper Shells

House Trucks

House Buses

Trailers

Cycles

Mark Hansen

Sailboats

Houseboats

Introduction

FOSTER HUNTINGTON QUIT HIS design job with Ralph Lauren in New York in August 2011 and moved into a camper. Since then, he has put in 80,000 miles driving around the west — writing a book, camping, and surfing.

Capucine Trochet, a 30-year-old French woman, left Marseille in her small sailboat in November 2011, and, with no engine or GPS, sailed 1,500 miles to the Canary Islands.

Jim Bob and Candice Salazar quit making high mortgage payments, sold their home in Texas, and now live, with their two children, in a family-remodeled school bus.

Muriel Chvatal left behind "…the noise of the city [and] rediscovered the music of the land — and the water…" when she moved to a houseboat on an English canal near Stonehenge.

What do all these people have in common?

They have chosen to build and inhabit homes that are tiny and mobile. They don't pay rent to a landlord, nor do they have lifetime mortgage obligations to a bank.

There are two main categories of mobile tiny homes in this book, with these sub-categories:

Wheels:

- 7 vans
- 11 pickup trucks with camper shells
- 7 house trucks
- 8 school buses
- 26 trailers
- 4 cycles

Water:

- 16 sailboats
- 7 houseboats
- 1 tugboat

There are some 90 tiny homes here, either rolling on the road or floating on the water. About half of these homes are lived in full time; the other half are used part time, or for trips of varying lengths upon life's highways and waterways.

A few examples:

- An English artist who has built a tiny home on the back of a 1959 French army truck
- A 72-year-old Swedish sailor who is building a 10-foot sailboat and plans to circumnavigate the globe. He's already sailed around the world solo.
- Further adventures of Swedish welder Henrick Lindström (his boat is in *Tiny Homes*), sailing with his girlfriend from Baja California to the South Seas and then to New Zealand

- A French circus wagon home on the road
- Two ski bums (a couple) and their winter camper/home
- The Moron Brothers, two good-ole-boy Kentucky bluegrass musicians who drift along the Kentucky River in a shanty boat, fishing, eating, telling jokes, and playing some really good bluegrass
- Sisters on the Fly, a group of over 1,000 women who have vintage trailers and go fly fishing and horseback riding and sit around campfires in campouts, just us girls
- Bruce Baillie's 23,000-mile trip from British Columbia to South America and back on a 1969 Moto Guzzi motorcycle
- A beautifully crafted shanty boat moored on a wooded waterfront in the UK

- Drew and Deb McVittie's 35-year-old, 58´-long tugboat home in British Columbia
- The Vaka Moana sailing canoes from the South Pacific. Three of these 66´ catamarans sailed into our bay here in 2011, and our local fishermen visited them and learned of their mission with the Pacific Ocean. They're navigating by the stars.
- A high-speed asymmetrical catamaran, a "Proa," that recently crossed the Pacific, from San Francisco to the Marquesas Islands

This is our latest book on owner-created homes, which started with *Shelter* in 1973, followed by *Home Work,* then *Builders of the Pacific Coast,* then *Tiny Homes*—all graphic-intensive books depicting innovative design, handmade building, and independent living.

This book is a continuation of *Tiny Homes,* here with 21st century nomadic living. There are some 1,100 photos, along with accompanying stories and descriptions of the different homes.

Come along with us in this tour of simple living and free spirits—rolling, floating, riding, rambling, wandering, exploring—moving.

Ongoing information: We are continuing the theme of this book, along with our other building books online, at ***www.TheShelterBlog.com***. We encourage you to send us photos and descriptions of mobile homes as well as other forms of homemade shelter. *(See p. 213 for details.)*

WHEELS

The Thomas J. Nugget Westfalia

Derek Quessenberry

THE VW WESTFALIA IS AN iconic vehicle, and to me, Thomas J. Nugget, or Nuggs for short, is my symbol of freedom. Nuggs is a 1989 Volkswagen Vanagon Westfalia camper van. He is in incredible condition and is equipped with a 2,200 cc, 2.2 L Subaru engine, built-in propane tank, two-burner stove top, thermostat-controlled furnace, a 12-gallon water tank, sink, roof-mounted solar panel, a refrigerator/freezer, two full-size beds, a swing-out table, and lots and lots of storage.

Westfalia camper vans have an amazing following. If you think the Jeep Wrangler wave is cool, then you'll love the peace sign Westy wave. They are certainly the ultimate adventure rig and are backed by a fun-loving and easygoing subculture.

"...a 1989 Volkswagen Vanagon Westfalia camper van."

Nuggs is named after my ancestors Thomas and John Quesenberry, but his nickname, Nuggs, is, well, a tribute to my inner hippie. Thomas Quesenberry left Europe to seek a new life in the colony of Virginia in 1624. After 21 years of colonial life, he returned to England, but his son John stayed. They represent bravery in the name of freedom and adventure, and in a sense, that is what Nuggs represents to me. He encourages me to look beyond that mundane 9-to-5 and live my life as a wonderful adventure. Nuggs is my escape from the cold grip of modern corporate society. Granted, I do love many aspects of my career as a software engineer in San Francisco, but I would much rather be out on the open road with Nuggs, connecting with nature, shooting photographs, camping with friends, and exploring all that I possibly can.

"...my symbol of freedom."

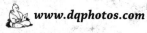
www.dqphotos.com

Chrissy Glover and Derek at the fold-out table

Derek with hiking buddy Chris Borgard at Banff National Park in Alberta, Canada

"...encourages me to live my life as a wonderful adventure."

Vagabond Surfer Van
Jonathan Banks

AFTER SEVERAL SEA voyages by sailboat, in 2009 I enrolled in a two-year boatbuilding course in Pembrokeshire, West Wales. I was lured by the prospect of learning a craft revolving around the sea, the chance to live the life of a gypsy vagabond and the opportunity to surf in one of Britain's best and least crowded surfing areas.

It was obvious that living in a van would mean paying no rent, the chance to explore the coastline and its many bays, and to wake up in a new place of my choosing every day. And I realized that if I wanted to live in my van, it would have to be warm, secure, low key, and comfortable; in essence a recreation of my old home, but on wheels.

I bought myself an old parcel force van, with no windows in the sides or back, and commenced to build a rollin' beach shack. Most of the construction wood came

from skips (dumpsters); the tongue and groove was salvaged from an old shop, sanded, and painted panel by panel. The insulation was 2-inch Kingspan (*rigid insulation*) from a derelict house, and the cupboard doors were all made from driftwood. Even the white paint came from skips.

My father-in-law, who has lived in a van for thirty years, provided the wood-burning stove — which was fueled by off-cuts from driftwood. I had one large leisure battery for the lights, although I used mostly lanterns, and one 20 kg bottle of gas, which lasted a whole year. Water was plumbed in from a 5-gallon bottle. Two skylights provided natural light. A large compartment under the bed provided space for two surf-boards and a plastic box for wetsuits.

As my daily classes finished at 3.30 I had plenty of time to go exploring around the coast. Many nights I'd be the first person in the water, and then would be sitting in my van watching the sunset over the sea, eating dinner as the first after-work crew arrived. Since it's light until 11 p.m. in June, I'd often go back in for another

surf after everyone had gone home.

Many surf spots in Pembroke-shire are quite remote, and the local population quite small. It's not uncommon to have only seagulls or a seal for company (sounds cheesy but it's true in some places!).

During winter, coming back to a warm van, making tea, and being heated by a wood-burning stove, whilst still within view of the sea, sure beat getting changed in a cold blustery car park and driving home with all the heaters on full blast. Many nights in the winter I'd park in a lay-by on the cliffs, under-neath wind-sculpted trees, and be rocked to sleep by a south-westerly gale, kept warm by my trusty wood burner. There's nothing like the hammer of rain and wind on the roof of a van a few feet above your head, whilst you're snug and dry, knowing that in the morning you'll wake up to waves.

Being near the sea at night, I'd lie in bed and hear the roll of the ocean and know that as soon as the sun came up, I'd be the first person in the water.

After my course was up, I sold the van to a couple in the Midlands, far from the sea. I couldn't help but feel guilty

that I'd packed my faithful old beach truck off to live inland, in a *city*. The only consolation was that she would no longer have her metal sides blasted daily by salt-laden winds and crapped on by seagulls.

Addendum: My wife and I are now living in Singapore, which is about as far from our old life as you can get. Tiny homes have a whole different meaning here and come with non-tiny prices! Being in Singapore, a big neon megatropolis where the sky is orange at night, sure makes me miss those lonely slow Atlantic sunsets and the cry of the last gull.... ah well, surf trips to Lombok (*Indonesia*) to look forward to...gonna get myself another big old van again someday; that life sure was fun.

"Most of the construction wood came from skips (dumpsters)."

> "I was lured by...the chance to live the life of a gypsy vagabond and the opportunity to surf in one of Britain's best and least crowded surfing areas."

> "There's nothing like the hammer of rain and wind on the roof of a van a few feet above your head, whilst you're snug and dry, knowing that in the morning you'll wake up to waves."

"A large compartment under the bed provided space for two surfboards and a plastic box for wetsuits."

Lloyd House's Van Revisited

Combination desk/counter/dining table folds up when not in use. When we had dinner, I sat on the bed, Lloyd pulled up a chair.

I MEET THE BUILDER OF MY DREAMS (after 40+ years of documenting builders and their work) and his name is Lloyd — *pause* — H-o-u-s-e. Cosmic or what? (I've written this before.)

Plus we get along together. Like my friend Louie, we're in the same age bracket, so we have references to a very different world. Almost everyone in my life is younger, so it's rare and wonderful to have these old guys who are tuned into the same things nowadays.

On my first photo trip to British Columbia in 2005, a number of Lloyd's buildings just stopped me in my tracks. Stefan's house, the sauna…"Oh yes!" And I'd sit down and enjoy the view before unloading cameras. Everything he did looked right, and impeccably crafted.

Lloyd is the primary builder in *Builders of the Pacific Coast.* By the time we got around to *Tiny Homes,* he'd walked away from his cliff-hanging seaside homestead and converted a 1990 Ford Econoline van into an exquisite

75 sq. ft. home. Michael McNamara photographed it for *Tiny Homes,* but I didn't see it until I was on a book tour in April 2012, and dropped in on Lloyd in his tiny home.

We hung out for a while, catching up. It was a cold late afternoon, and the fire in the little stove he'd built out of a 5-gallon propane tank gave out heat and cheerfulness. This place *felt* so good.

In addition to a brilliant design, it's got two unique things going for it.

1. The curved roof, which gives you a feeling of openness, expansion (the opposite is a flat roof). There's Mylar insulation in the ceiling that reflects the rugs on the floor

2. There are (openable) polycarbonate windows all around — at eye level when you are standing. This brings the outside in and, again, makes the space feel open and unconstrained.

Just before it got dark, Lloyd gathered salad greens and vegetables in the greenhouse, and we had dinner.

View of the outside trees (at eye level) brings outside in.

There are (openable) polycarbonate windows all around—this brings the outside in...

Lloyd is the primary builder in Builders of the Pacific Coast.

Lloyd welded up wood stove from 5-gallon propane tank. Handle slides up and down on curved upright rod to adjust door from open to tightly closed. Ash catcher is old wok.

Compact kitchen, propane-powered 2-burner stove. Dishes, knives above sink. Mirror (I think) for Feng Shui effect.

The curved roof...gives you a feeling of openness...

Three little buildings around Lloyd's van

Sprinter Van Conversion

Paul Jensen

ALEX IS A CALIFORNIA resident who works at a hospital about a half hour from his home. The job frequently requires him to be on close call. He is paid a per diem for that. Instead of continuing to stay in hotels, he bought a used 2005 Dodge Sprinter for a bit more than what the yearly per diem is. The van will be his "home" while on call, and he will also use it for adventures on the beaches, or the mountains.

Alex had a long look at similar Sprinter conversions I've done, so we started a conversation about his wants and needs, then refined that list to keep the budget from blowing out with stuff he likely didn't need. Our design plan was to create a very nice steel tent. Simple, elegant, and functional.

A 6-gallon water system is gravity fed into a sink that drains over a tire.

LED lighting, both white and red, illuminates the interior. Refrigeration is an ice chest, and cooking is done on propane camping stoves.

The bed is a pair of inflatable camping pads that go on the floor at night, then strap to the wall during the day. There are hammock-hanging rings bolted to the roof. Maximum usable floor space is a priority.

The cabinets are fir plywood, and the drawers are white pine. The drawer pulls and slide latches are walnut. The ceiling is cork, and the floor is bamboo. The wood wall is sliced and planed 2×4 fir.

Stainless steel drop-down tables are on each of the rear doors. Another lift-up stainless table is next to the sink, and a three-person lift-up wood table is behind the driver's seat. Both front seats swivel.

A clip-on awning extends the living space outdoors.

The work took place at my shop in Olympia, Washington and took about a month. The conversion cost was around $7,000 total.

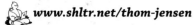 **www.shltr.net/thom-jensen**

"Our design plan was to create a very nice steel tent. Simple, elegant, and functional."

"Stainless steel drop-down tables are on each of the rear doors."

"The bed is a pair of inflatable camping pads that go on the floor at night, then strap to the wall during the day."

"The conversion cost was around $7,000 total."

"The ceiling is cork, and the floor is bamboo."

Amerikanomade
Diego Mariot & Veronica Bavaro

Two Argentinian Gypsies on the Road for 6 Years in 1965 VW Van

These two have a beautiful, interesting, exciting life.

In 2009, I spent a couple of weeks on the Osa Peninsula, which is in the southwest corner of Costa Rica, on the Pacific Ocean. I took a swim one morning, around the rocky point south of where I was staying (at a friend's house in the jungle). When I came up on the sandy beach, I spotted this van, and was fascinated to meet Diego Mariot and Veronica Bavaro from Argentina.

Diego started out on a road trip in the van three years earlier, and on the fifth day of the trip met his soul mate Veronica, and they'd been traveling together ever since. Their main source of income came from Veronica's handmade necklaces, bracelets, and earrings. They looked like beadwork, but were woven knots. (I don't know what the correct name is for this craft.) They are lovely things.

Every square inch of the van inside was decorated, and was neat and orderly and intelligently designed. Diego does all the mechanics on the van.

Parts are sometimes hard to get, he says. They are vegetarians. At that point, they had spent two months in Argentina, 20 days in Bolivia, six months in Brazil, 1½ years in Venezuela, two months in Columbia, nine months in Panama, and had been in Costa Rica for two weeks and were planning to stay three months. Then on to Mexico "… for six months or three years."

They didn't speak English, so I gathered this info in Spanish.

These two have a beautiful, interesting, exciting life.

———

Now, three years later, they are apparently still out there. Here's the link to their blog (in Spanish): **www.shltr.net/thom-amerikano**

By the way, to Latinos, America does not mean just the United States. It also refers to Central and South America.

Diego and Veronica were fascinated by Home Work. I left it with them overnight. We had immediate rapport as soon as they saw the book.

You VW van fans will love this: Diego showing off the "air conditioning."

Their main source of income comes from Veronica's handmade necklaces, bracelets, and earrings.

Fish being caught on beach that day

View of beach from van

Every square inch of the van inside is decorated, and it's neat and orderly and intelligently designed.

My notebook from 6-week trip to Costa Rica and Panama

Nomad Oasis

Dipa Vasudeva Das

EARTH SHIP IS A COMMON delivery van transformed into a new form by the Divine Creativity Factory. The project has several components:

- Handmade wood stove, built small for year-round living anywhere
- Dipa Mandir: Temple of Light
- Pilgrimage Traveling Photo Gallery. Photo exhibition outdoors anywhere anytime.
- Tearoom/restaurant/bakery treats our revered visitors well. Our motto is: Don't panic — drink and eat organic.
- Sunlight Bioscope/solar cinema. How else would this part of the project run but on solar energy? We present movies about natural and eco-bio issues.
- A mobile photo gallery/tearoom/audio-video studio/solar cinema on the go

www.DivineFactory.net/cs/earthship

"Mobile photo gallery/tearoom/ audio-video studio/solar cinema on the go"

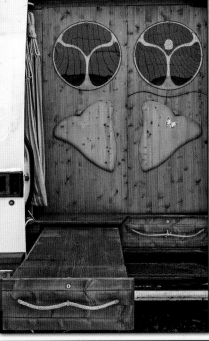

Van Studio
Beth Ireland

"I renovated a Chevy Express cargo van into a live/workshop space and traveled the country teaching woodworking from the van for one year."

"The shop has a lathe that pulls out to 50 inches . . . (a) band saw, grinder, clamps, extension cords, hand tools . . ."

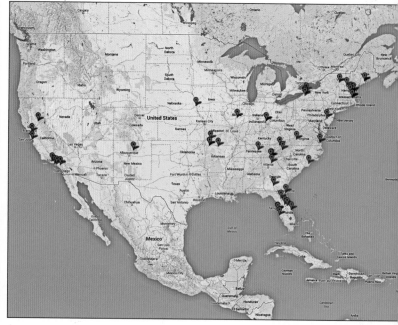

"The van renovation cost about $300."

Your book *Shelter* has impacted my life in many ways. I bought it in college in 1979 and have always carried it around like a sacred text. (It's now in shreds and I've made an envelope to keep it in.)

"Turning Around America" is a project that was started in 2010. I renovated a Chevy Express cargo van into a live/workshop space and traveled the country teaching woodworking from the van for one year.

While I traveled, fellow artist Jenn Moller created an interactive website that allowed people to follow my progress. We found that having a mobile workspace allowed us to reach 3,000 people. The project was so successful that we are now designing other forms of mobile classroom/ artist spaces, in a project we call "Sanctuary."

The van renovation cost about $300. The living space is surprisingly roomy with two bins, three drawers, and cupboard space for clothes. Storage for cooking utensils and propane burner, and shelves for shoes, books, and miscellaneous. There is a desk that folds down into a book-making studio.

There is a double bed with a Tempurpedic mattress (under which I store paper — flat).

For airflow, I have a solar vent and a window vent over the bed. I run all electronics off a power pack charged from a solar panel.

The shop has a lathe that pulls out to 50 inches with a storage box behind. There is space to hold three bins, a toolbox, band saw, grinder, clamps, extension cords, hand tools, and an extra lathe when necessary.

During the year, I taught at many elementary schools. The kids always wanted to see the van. When looking in the door of the living space, one of them would invariably say, "Wait a minute. How do you sleep and drive at the same time?"

 www.TurningAroundAmerica.com

"There is a desk that folds down into a book-making studio."

La Cam'bane de Yogan et Menthé

Yogan

WE CALL THIS HOUSE *cam'bane* from *camion* (truck) and *cabane* (cabin).

Three of us were living in our trucks in the woods of Périgord, near Sarlat (France). We decided to build this small "dock," so that we could connect our trucks to it. We then used the trucks as bedrooms and the dock as a living space with kitchen, office, bathroom, etc., of 15 square meters.

The frame of the dock is chestnut, and the walls are made of old hotel doors. Insulation is sheep's wool from a mattress, and the exterior finish is clay. We use solar energy for lights and music with a 220-watt electric cable that came from an old Hoover vacuum cleaner. For more power, we have a diesel generator powered with old oil from French fries and duck grease of Périgord, very local!! At times, we use batteries from our trucks.

The trucks are connected to the dock with an old foam mattress protected from the rain. It only takes us a few minutes to make the connection (we use the trucks every day for work).

There is a big wood heater, hot in five minutes when wood is not wet!! Ha-ha.

It took about three weeks to build and we spent about 500 euros on materials.

We hope to build another one like this in a different part of France for travel and work.

Yogan: *yogan.over-blog.com*
Menthé: *menthedesbois.blogspot.fr*

18

"We use solar energy for lights and music..."

"We decided to build this small 'dock,' so that we could connect our trucks to it."

Mikey's Snowchaser

Evan Kahn

> "He then built a custom camper to fit the truck bed, with a liftable top."

MIKE BASICH WAS A FEATURED builder in our last book, *Tiny Homes*. Each year he makes a pilgrimage to Alaska in the beginning of the spring to finish off his year of snowboarding.

Snowmobiles are essential in Alaska, and carrying a snowmobile requires a trailer if you want to utilize the bed of the truck for sleeping. But having a trailer means spending a long time in the chains checkpoint going into the mountains, so Mike decided to build a pop-up camper.

He bought a 1999 Dodge Ram and started by cutting out the back of the cab and fitting a massive custom roll bar made out of 2″ square tubing where the end of the cab used to be. He then built a custom camper to fit the truck bed, with a liftable top. This way, after the snowmobile was secured, the roof could raise to allow for a more comfortable living space. Mike joined the bed to the truck body, which made for a more stable ride. Swiveling pilot seats were added, as well as custom cabinetry and LED lighting, to make the space more comfortable.

The truck uses two 400 lb. hydraulic struts to lift the bed. Flexible nylon sheeting covers the openings when the bed is lifted. Mike printed a photo he took of a mountain range in Alaska on the nylon sheet. He then attached it to the bed and bottom of the ramp so that when the ramp is lifted, he's still protected from the elements.

It took him around 17 days, working 15–17 hours a day, to complete the truck; four days alone went into fitting the roll bar to the truck body.

The truck runs on a biodiesel mix whenever he has access to it, and he has plans for a custom grease kit in the future.

You never know what Mike's going to be doing next: building a one-off truck, assembling a ski lift on his property, or sailing around the Pacific Ocean in his recently-acquired 1958 wooden sailboat.

 www.241-usa.com

Mike backs the truck up against a snowbank to load and unload the snowmobile.

"The truck uses two 400 lb. hydraulic struts to lift the bed."

"The truck runs on a biodiesel mix whenever he has access to it . . ."

Home Is Where You Park It

Foster Huntington

I spent 12 years traveling in Baja, mostly in the south. I first had a Baja Bug (converted VW sedan), then two Toyota Tacoma 4×4s. As with all Baja-roamers, I obsessed about desert vehicles. Everyone has a different rig.

Foster's rig is the best thing I've seen for desert roaming and surfing. He stopped by one afternoon on his way north to Oregon, and Evan and I checked out his Toyota-with-camper. The truck has been converted to a flatbed, the camper weighs only 1,000 pounds, and it's got lots of efficient standup space when the camper is raised. It can also be used in "stealth mode": you can sleep in it with the top down, and it doesn't look like anyone is in it. It's got all kinds of conveniences and well-thought-out details. Cost for new truck and camper was about 50K; not expensive when you consider the price of a home or a couple of years' paying rent. You've got a comfortable, convenient home that will go anywhere.

—LK

IN 2011, I QUIT MY corporate job, packed up my Manhattan apartment and moved into a 1987 VW Vanagon Syncro. I wanted to get back to living a simpler life and spend more time outdoors. A VW Syncro seemed like a great option. I found mine on a website called the Samba and bought it without ever seeing it. I was the second owner.

The original owner, also a Portland, Oregon native, had swapped out the original VW waterboxer engine for a 2.0L Audi. With the help of some cabinets and build-outs courtesy of my Mom and her boyfriend, I lived out of it for a year and a half and put about 60,000 miles on it. After a while, I got tired of the constant nagging breakdowns associated with living in a car with 340,000 miles on it and decided to get something newer.

In my travels, I'd come across many people that were original owners of Toyota-truck-based campers. Many of these rigs have been all over the place, from Alaska to Central America. I also based my decision on reliability: vehicles I saw Mexicans driving in Baja.

I started looking at options for truck campers and eventually decided that a flatbed-based camper would give me the most livable space and storage for a given size of truck.

I loved living on the road and wanted to get something that would last. I wanted something that felt more like a home than a place to sleep. I ordered the camper from Four Wheel Campers and had AT Overland do the conversion. It will last me decades.

Vital Statistics

Model: 2013 Toyota Tacoma Access cab with a flatbed four-wheel camper. V6, 6-speed transmission

Propane tank: 20 lb cylinder

Water tank: 20 gallons

Wiring: 12v and 110 wiring

Plumbing: Electric system with indoor and outdoor shower

Heating: 20,000 BTU forced-air propane heater with thermostat.

Solar: 160 watt fixed panel and 225 amp hours, deep-cycle marine batteries

Appliances: 80L compressor refrigerator and two-burner propane stove

Flooring: Slip-resistant composite flooring

Bed: King-size and a 6-foot guest bed

 www.ARestlessTransplant.com
www.FourWheelCampers.com
www.AdventureTrailers.com/camper.html

Quickupcamper™

Jay Baldwin

Jay and I go back over 40 years. We met in 1967 when he visited my homestead in Big Sur. Soon after, he introduced me to Stewart Brand, who was tinkering with the idea of doing something called The Whole Earth Catalog. *The next summer I got Jay a job as a design teacher at Pacific High School, a hippy high school in the Santa Cruz Mountains, above what is now called Silicon Valley.*

I led a program of building wooden domes for the kids, which, to say the least, were not successful at keeping rain outside. Jay designed, and he and his then-partner Kathleen built, a futuristic pipe-frame dome sheathed in nitrogen-filled vinyl pillows. Bucky Fuller visited, liked it, and got Jay to build one for him in Maine.

Jay went on to be the design editor on successive Whole Earth Catalogs *and magazines, and has taught design courses at Sonoma State University, San Francisco Institute of Architecture and at California College of the Arts. There's a complete review of his career in Wikipedia.*

I think this is Jay's best design yet; and I say this as a pickup-truck-with-camper-shell guy for the last 25 years. A key feature is that it's aerodynamic while on the road. Years of experience and persistent attention to detail and quality here. Angel investors should get it into production!

–LK

N 2001, LIZ AND I NEEDED TO replace our well-worn 1973 Toyota Chinook pop top camper, but we couldn't find a sturdy, affordable RV that got good mileage, handled well, was crosswind-stable, and cruised easily, like a car. It couldn't have any canvas portions because such vehicles are not approved in Yellowstone and other parks with bears. A good RV should also fit urban parking facilities, allowing visitors to explore interesting cities. It should also be legal to park (closed) where RV parking is not allowed.

I sketched an RV that would provide all that. Ford helped us with an F150 long-bed pickup with automatic transmission, air conditioning, heavy-duty radiator, one-ton capacity and the highest gear ratio. The F150 has been the world's best-selling vehicle for more than 30 years, assuring parts and service available anywhere. A full-scale plywood pickup cargo bed and cardboard bodywork helped us develop the aerodynamics, the best interior layout, and a balanced chassis. The arch profile of the interior (fig. 1) showed that my concept would be roomy and light-filled.

We took on an intern from CCA (California College of the Arts) where

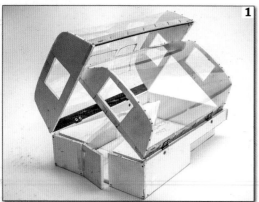

In Death Valley

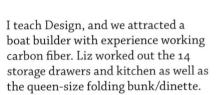

Bunk is about 5′5″ × 7′6″, with more than 4 feet of headroom. It does not interfere with the kitchen, fridge, Portapotti™, or block any drawers.

Headroom is at least 6 feet 4 inches throughout.

I teach Design, and we attracted a boat builder with experience working carbon fiber. Liz worked out the 14 storage drawers and kitchen as well as the queen-size folding bunk/dinette.

It took nine months to make the molds, lay up the shells, and make the windows. Liz designed and built the entire interior, which remains fully useful when the bunk is deployed. Eleven years of varied use has shown the rig to work well. Of course, there have been a few minor opportunities for improvement; that's what prototypes are for. Only one matter has yet to be solved: we have not yet found a cabin heater small enough to deal with our highly insulated Quickupcamper!

Patented, 2002.

www.quickupcamper.com

"**A good RV should also fit urban parking facilities, allowing visitors to explore interesting cities. It should also be legal to park (closed) where RV parking is not allowed.**"

Casual Turtle Campers

Peter Pavlowich

The idea for Casual Turtle Campers was conceived in the summer of 2010. On a road trip to Colorado, I noticed an abundance of truck campers but a profound lack of variety or style. As a Wood Construction and Design graduate from the University of Idaho, I knew I could design and build a simple and attractive alternative to the big, heavy, white boxes I seemed to see everywhere. Over the next few years, I brought together ideas and drew up plans for what would eventually become the design for Casual Turtle Campers.

I knew that I wanted them to be decidedly small and *simple*. As a fan of the small living movement in general, I knew there were people out there that felt the same way. I also wanted them to be unique; simple wooden campers had certainly been done. Arched roofs aren't rare, but I had never seen a camper with a domed roof, that is to say, arched in both axes. This makes for a strong, practical roof that also enhances the aesthetics of the camper. And being lightweight (910 lbs. as pictured), they can be built for use with almost any pickup.

At 6′2″, I can't stand up straight inside my campers. I can, however, sit and enjoy a Fort Collins craft beer with great ease. And that's really the idea: a comfortable place to get out of the rain, have a bite, read a book, and sleep at night. And in the morning, grab a cup, decide where-to and what-for, and take off without having to tear down, collapse a pop-up roof, or hitch up a trailer. The idea of simplicity is meant not only to describe Casual Turtle Campers, but also their use.

 *www.CasualTurtleCampers.com*

"I knew I could design and build a simple and attractive alternative to the big, heavy, white boxes . . ."

"I knew that I wanted them to be decidedly small and simple."

"...that's really the idea: a comfortable place to get out of the rain, have a bite, read a book, and sleep at night."

"...being lightweight (910 lbs. as pictured), they can be built for use with almost any pickup."

Jay's Lightweight Camper Shell

Jay Nelson

Jay is a San Francisco artist (painter) and surfer, and he has built a number of customized lightweight vehicles. Four of them are featured in Tiny Homes (pp. 180–181): a Honda Civic camper, an 8-foot covered dinghy, an electric car with bicycle wheels, and a surfer's motor scooter. This is his latest creation.

> "It's on a 1986 long-bed Toyota truck that I converted to a flatbed..."

T**HIS IS MY NEWEST CAMPER**; I finished it at the beginning of the year. It's on a 1986 long-bed Toyota truck that I converted to a flatbed; the shell can slide off by removing four bolts.

It has a basic kitchen: a single burner, sink with water pump, and a cooler. The bed cantilevers over the cab; it's 6 feet long and folds into a sofa. The frame is all recycled redwood; the skin is ¼″ plywood with bio-epoxy resin and fiberglass. It's insulated and weighs around 400 pounds.

 www.JayNelsonArt.com

28

"It has a basic kitchen: a single burner, sink with water pump, and a cooler. The bed cantilevers over the cab; it's 6 feet long and folds into a sofa."

Old-Style Pickup Truck Camper

Nels & Cathy Norene

2004 Toyota Tacoma extended-cab pickup truck, with automatic transmission and the smaller of the 4-cylinder engines. I'm a veteran surfer living in Southern California with a wife and dog. We do a lot of our own work on and around the house we live in. Secure material and recreational equipment storage and transportation are the rule locally. Travel tends to be to destinations hours away from home, with camping or fishing equipment.

Lloyd,

Like so many others, I've been enjoying your work since early Shelter days, and have been enjoying the recent books.... I was a huge fan of "Roll Your Own" back in the day. I spent time living out of a van both traveling and "in place" and have spent thousands of days on the road or camping in various manners....

My wife and I are in our 50s now, and with that many miles under the hood, so to speak, we've gone through a few phases. We don't live in the vehicle, a 2004 Toyota Tacoma with automatic transmission and the smaller of the 4-cylinder engines. But as with people who do live in tiny houses or vehicles, we tend to "live outside" our house. We still evaluate and seek the ultimate vehicle, but this has been doing it for us for a few years now.

–Nels and Cathy

After literally a year or so of agonizing research we decided on a cab over Bel-Air Camper Shell. It's very old school, like the smaller shell I had on a 1973 Ford Courier truck back in the 1970s and 1980s. Custom-built, insulated, two overhead lights, two sliding windows on the sides, a pass-through up front, and a window on the door.

I cut a sheet of quarter-inch plywood to give it a lightweight floor, figuring to replace it periodically. It's still going strong four years later.

Another view. At this point we take nearly as much stuff for one night as 7 or 14. The camping gear remains the same. The only difference is clothing, depending on the type of events we might encounter. On long trips to the Pacific Northwest we might need to pack clothes for formal events, everyday wear in urban places, and camp clothes for warm and cold camping. Deserts can be hot, high altitude cold, and beaches cool. On an overnight trip like this not much is required beyond a pair of long pants and a sweatshirt.

Interior. My wife Cathy made curtains for camping. These have some blackout material on the back, which keeps it nice and dark inside and blocks light from escaping. It has proven to keep the inside much, much warmer in very cold temperatures. We hang them on removable 3M wall hooks that we had used to hold holiday decorations. We bought two memory foam mattresses on sale for about $50 total, and Cathy took an old flannel sheet set and sewed a cover that closes with a few buttons. It's machine washable.... We roll the mattress up and use sleeping bag straps to hold it.

Campground living. We got one of those polypropylene rugs that you can just hose off when you get home. It keeps dust down and little rocks out, and makes it easier on the dog and our feet. A soft leash makes use of the mounting hole for a trailer hitch.

Battery-operated Christmas lights. LED lights are best, minimal draw. Fantastic inside or outside.

This was taken on an Eastern Sierra camping trip with our dog Cordi. We decided to get a decent tent for sleeping this time as we knew we would be leaving camp for fishing and other adventures and didn't want to have to break camp every time. It was sunny and warm during the day and cold at night, so some daytime was spent in the shade inside and some nighttime lounging was done in there to stay warm.

Million-dollar view of the Oregon coast. My cousins had rented a fantastic house, but I have a lot of cousins and the house was full. Complete comfort.

Pop-up Camper for Two
Lew Lewandowski & Krystal Allen

DURING THE PAST fifty years, most of my camping has involved canvas: a kid's army surplus backyard pup tent, a canvas sun-roofed, VW window bus, a tipi at 9,000 feet on the Colorado Continental Divide, a pop-up Westphalia VW camper, and later on, an SUV-hugging tent. Canvas is lightweight, brightens with sunlight during the day, and glows from within at night.

As a young carpenter, I spent a few years living in my VW van while working various small remodeling jobs in Colorado, Nevada, and California. I had enough room for my camping gear, my carpentry tools, and a dog or two. Winters were a little hard, but I'd head for the coast to enjoy the beach when the snow got too deep. Along the way, I'd sometimes find a garage, basement, or backyard shed that I could convert to a comfortable living space in a short-term exchange for rent.

Life was simple, and generally good, but the Westphalia camper was totally underpowered, especially when filled with all my gear. Even then, I couldn't haul much more than 5 gallons of water, which severely limited desert trips. There was little, or

no, heat during the winter. In addition, gas mileage was usually less than 20 mpg because the weak engine needed to be constantly floored. Getting stuck in mud and snow was pretty common too, because it was only 2-wheel drive, and I was usually alone.

But camping life changed once I was married to Krystal Allen, a plein-air landscape painter, with all her additional gear that maxed out the poor VW. Expensive engine rebuilds were happening on a regular basis, and brake jobs were

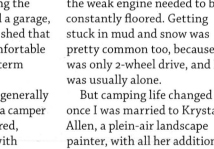

eating up weekends when we could have been camping. We eventually bought an SUV, using a specially made tent that extended over the rear hatch of the truck. It added 100 sq. ft. to our camping set-up, giving us plenty of room for our gear and dog while we slept in the back of the SUV. However, this new arrangement turned out to be a problem in high winds and freezing temperatures — we needed to upgrade so we could camp in less-than-ideal conditions.

As an artist, Krystal needs

to be camping for days or even weeks at a time. Our camp must be comfortable and quick to set up and take down, and our vehicle must be reliable and capable of taking her to remote locations (and back out again).

A 4WD pickup with a camper can be a good home on wheels. However, a standard shell is too small and cramped, while a cab-over is too tall and top-heavy to travel well off-road. We researched different options and decided on a Palomino Bronco — a canvas-sided, pop-up camper. This lightweight

"...a pretty good compromise between comfort and capability..."

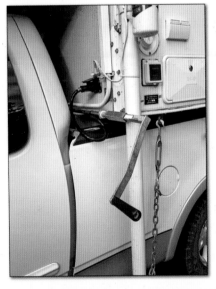

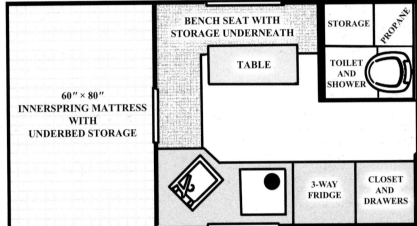

BENCH SEAT WITH STORAGE UNDERNEATH

STORAGE

PROPANE

TABLE

TOILET AND SHOWER

60" × 80" INNERSPRING MATTRESS WITH UNDERBED STORAGE

3-WAY FRIDGE

CLOSET AND DRAWERS

truck camper features a pop-up roof that raises with an easy-to-operate crank system, creating a spacious interior with full stand-up room and lots of convenient features. The Bronco's low-profile design delivers better fuel efficiency and on- or off-the-road handling.

Remote-controlled electric jacks effortlessly lower/lift the camper from the pickup bed, enabling the truck to be used for other purposes between trips. Once camped, the hand crank quickly raises the roof, creating a 6′4″ ceiling surrounded by screened vinyl windows. The bed is a queen-sized Serta mattress, with storage below. Twenty-two gallons of water are delivered to the sink, indoor and outdoor showers, and flush toilet. A twenty-pound propane tank feeds the hot water heater, a 3-burner stovetop, a powerful wall heater, and additionally runs the 3-cubic-foot refrigerator, which can also operate on either AC or 12v from the two deep-cycle batteries.

We feel like we've achieved a pretty good compromise between comfort and capability, and we're ready to camp somewhere down the road....

Yucca Dance ©2008 Krystal Allen   18 × 24 inches, oil on canvas

While Krystal paints, I fish for dinner.

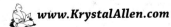

www.KrystalAllen.com

A Day in the Life of Two Ski Bums

Chris & Cat

A DAY IN THE LIFE OF TWO ski bums living in a home-built camper goes something like this:

First thing every morning one of us (usually Chris) spends a few minutes wiping away frozen droplets and icicles of condensation that form along the aluminum tubing frame of the camper's ceiling. While this

is being done, the other one of us (usually Cat) reaches across with her feet and turns on the catalytic heater with her toes.

Once the tiny space is warmed up to around 0°C / 32°F. (less than five minutes), we dress and eat breakfast. We have a pee-bucket with a toilet seat, but most of our business is either done outside in the forest or in some local facilities. We have a camping stove for cooking with a computer fan mounted in the wall above to exhale humidity. The fan isn't strong enough, so we always open the door when cooking, or we cook outside.

Once we're ready for our day of touring, we step outside (often parked within a few steps of the trailhead) and pull our skis and poles out of the ski storage. The asymmetrical peaked roof (dubbed the "space ship" by some) gives our winter home a

unique character. Although we don't always have the energy to raise the roof (especially after a day of touring when it's cold out), we both love the extra space and the homey feeling that our pop-top loft gives us.

The camper is well built and

survived a winter rollover accident with no damage. To minimize weight, the removable camper shell (600 lbs, no floor) is made with: 1.5″ aluminum tubing, aluminum siding, blue insulation foam, and 4mm plywood (interior). It mounts

> "To date, our camper adventures have taken us from Quebec, through BC, the Yukon, the Northwest Territories…and to…Smithers, BC."

> "…we both love the extra space and the homey feeling that our pop-top loft gives us."

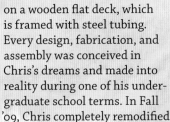

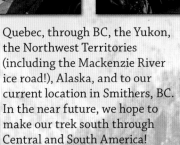

on a wooden flat deck, which is framed with steel tubing. Every design, fabrication, and assembly was conceived in Chris's dreams and made into reality during one of his under-graduate school terms. In Fall '09, Chris completely remodified the pop-top mechanism from the original flat raising roof with canvas fabric walls, to the current A-frame roof with removable hard-shell-insulated walls for winter.

To date, our camper adventures have taken us from Quebec, through BC, the Yukon, the Northwest Territories (including the Mackenzie River ice road!), Alaska, and to our current location in Smithers, BC. In the near future, we hope to make our trek south through Central and South America!

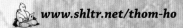 **www.shltr.net/thom-ho**

35

Rick's Rustic Nomad Rig

Rick Auerbach

In Tiny Homes, *we did four pages of Rick's photos, titled "American Nomad Rigs," of house buses, house trucks, vans, and campers inhabited by musicians, craftspeople, artists, and nomads of the counterculture. As we were finishing up this book, Rick sent us these photos of his own road rig. You'd never guess at the color and richness of the interior by looking at the truck from the outside.*

I BELIEVE THE PULL TO SEE and know the beauty, wonders, and strangeness over the next hill is an ancient human need burned into our DNA from the time our ancestors flowed across and out of Africa. Though only one of many components driving our species' migrations, the heartbeat of this wanderlust has continued to pulse though ger, tipi, and vardo across the millennia into the present.

When building my small cabin on a '63 Chevy pickup in 1978, I couldn't have imagined I'd still be traveling in its welcoming simplicity 35 years later. But every spring an ancient stirring finds me and the rig out on the back roads and into the wilderness beyond, a journey both joyous and practical for a working musician and nature photographer.

Part of an extended family of musicians and artisans that gathers in our rigs at friends' hillside farms and up in the mountains, we work on our crafts and practice our songs around the fire, preparing to perform and vend at the many high summer festivals, fairs, and gatherings throughout the West.

For 35 years I've been documenting handbuilt, traveling homes, taking thousands of photographs of hundreds of rigs, to this day endlessly inspired by the creativity of people who seek, like the birds overhead, to live on the wind.

" . . . every spring an ancient stirring finds me and the rig out on the back roads and into the wilderness beyond . . ."

"I believe the pull to see and know the beauty,
wonders, and strangeness over the next hill is
an ancient human need burned into our DNA..."

Wooden Camper Shell

Robert Van Vranken

"So it was just two middle-aged Buddhists driving across the country looking for a place to live."

Robert and Baerbel in Peacham, Vermont

"Automobiles are so industrially produced now, that people just don't think you can do anything handmade to them. Not so!"

I DESIGNED AND BUILT THE Camper Shell based on the little teardrop trailers — you know, the ones with the curved backs. In fact I almost bought one for the trip, but, due to the fact that I was sitting on my hands waiting for the world's slowest divorce to go through, I thought, what the heck, why don't I just build one of those little teardrops right onto the back of the truck?

The key was to keep it somewhat light (without using sheet metal, which I do not know how to work with) and to make it watertight. I used ⅛" thick marine mahogany plywood over a fir frame — glued and screwed together. Finished the exterior with the West System two-part marine epoxy. She didn't leak a drop, and performed beautifully at 65 mph. Comfy for two to sleep in — with tons of storage down below the sleeping deck.

So it was just two middle-aged Buddhists driving across the country looking for a place to live. I must say, however, that there was hardly a gas station, etc., we stopped at where someone did not come up and lay praises on our wooden camper. If I was single and young, I might have lived in this thing a long time.

It got lots of attention — owing, I think, to the curved shape, and the wood finish. Automobiles are so industrially produced now, that people just don't think you can do anything handmade to them. Not so!

 *www.RVVart.com*

The Roulotte
Yogan

"Laurine lives with very little money. She does not have a cell phone…"

"Many young people in France don't have money enough to rent an apartment or house, and more and more (mostly young) people like the idea of living in cabins in the country-side…"

Laurine with her horse Kinoa

From left: Menthé (red cap), Rémix, Laurine, Thomas, Rémi

Laurine came to spend the winter with us at "La Petite Chartreuse" (our collective in Périgord). All of us here live in our own cabins — me in the Cam'bane (*see pp. 18–19*), Menthé in the Philibert Delorme cabin, Paul in a little mower structure, and Rémix in the hexagonal mower cob house.

For Laurine we designed a *roulotte* (caravan). For 600 euros we bought an old *calèche* (horse-drawn carriage) in poor condition. We worked on it for two months; we replaced many rotted wood pieces with oak. We used Douglas fir for the structure and wall exterior, poplar for the interior, and for insulation a wool mattress from the dump. The roofing is recycled metal cut with a skill saw.

Laurine lives with very little money. She does not have a cell phone (in France there are more cell phones than people!), she doesn't have a car, and she moved here with her three horses — traveling 400 km from the French Pyrenees in 15 days. (She was motivated!) She likes to live simply (rare in this world).

The roulotte weighs about 900 kg — too heavy to be pulled by horses, so it will stay here at "La Petite Chartreuse." In France we don't have the right to build cabins for homes, and the *roulotte* was a good solution for the authorities (our four other cabins are not legal).

Many young people in France don't have money enough to rent an apartment or house, and more and more (mostly young) people like the idea of living in cabins in the country-side — which is a problem for society because we don't pay taxes or rent.

You can follow the evolution of "La Petite Chartreuse" at:

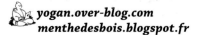

yogan.over-blog.com
menthedesbois.blogspot.fr

Federal House Truck

John Driscoll

THE INSPIRATION FOR THIS house truck came from an encounter in 1969 with a group of people living on the east side of Mount Hood (Oregon). They called themselves the Cooper Spur Gypsies. They were living in four or five house trucks and about the same number of converted buses. There was one truck that I particularly liked, a 1947 Mack 2-ton with a house built on a 16-ft. flatbed. It had a curved roof at the back that blended into twin peaks at the front.

> *"In 1972, with no formal carpenters' experience, but all of the confidence of a 23-year-old, I started framing...."*

In 1971, I bought a 1949 Federal 2-ton flatbed truck for $125.00. I replaced the worn-out engine, and transmission, rebuilt the brakes, and was off and running on a project that continues to this day.

My original design goals were relatively simple. Try to avoid building a square box; this is not as simple as it sounds on a truck chassis. A curved roof, 45-degree corners at the front, and a mitered wall at the back helped with this theme. In 1972, with no formal carpenter's experience, but all of the confidence of a 23-year-old, I started framing. Curved roof beams were laminated using ½-inch strips of white oak from a recycled water tower; wall framing is 2″ × 3″, ½-inch plywood on the outside, and ¼-inch plywood on the inside. All fasteners are either ring shank nails, or screws. Roof stringers are ¾ × ¾, and 1½ × ¾ alternately at 6 inches on center; ¼-inch plywood over the top, rolled aluminum at the sides, and plywood ribs with urethane foam at the complex curves at the front.

The entire roof structure is fiber glassed with the cloth wrapping on to the sidewalls a couple of inches. The entire roof is essentially one piece—light, but very strong. This is probably one of the reasons the truck is still around after 40 years, and 50,000 miles of travel.

By 1975, the exterior was finished as you see it in these pictures. The stained and beveled glass panels in the windows were rebuilt from broken windows purchased at junk stores. These have leaded frames that are reinforced with brass ribs. The front diamond window, and the back door glasses were custom-made from automobile safety plate with a bevel ground on them. The Dutch door was made from scratch, it's 6′2″ tall and 26″ wide—perfect scale for the truck.

We put in a counter, a marine alcohol stove, my grandmother's couch, and took off for Yosemite. The Federal was used in this form until 1983 when the complete interior (kitchen, bathroom, shower, etc.) was done. Also at this time the side mount, gas tanks, and storage boxes

came off, and the aluminum side boxes and boat tail at the rear were built.

> *"The boxes can carry a 14′ Zodiac inflatable boat, and a 40 hp Suzuki outboard, or a lot of camping gear and junk."*

A local traffic sign company supplied much of the recycled aluminum for the storage boxes. The boxes can carry a 14′ Zodiac inflatable boat, and a 40 hp Suzuki outboard, or a lot of camping gear and junk. At the right rear, under the kitchen, they hold a generator, water heater, and a forced-air gas furnace.

Starting at the back, the stairs, propane tank, 60-gallon grey water tank, 35-gallon black water tank, 30-gallon fresh water tank, 55-gallon main, and 20-gallon reserve gas tanks all ride between the frame rails under the bed.

Light weight for this vehicle is about 13,500 lbs., loaded about 15,000 lbs. It is 11 feet tall, but the center of gravity is very low, because all of the heavy components are under the bed. The secondary aluminum roof has a continuous ridge vent that cools the vehicle when it is in direct sunlight and prevents degradation of the fiberglass.

In 2005, I installed a 455 hp Pontiac engine (I finally managed to wear out the original 389). The new engine actually gets better mileage — 9.7 miles to the gallon on regular. In 2010, I installed new axles, and hubs with a hybrid 2005 F-550 disc brake system. 1949 trucks do not have adequate brakes for modern traffic, and speeds.

Over the years, the Federal has provided a great deal of entertainment for our family. If you don't like meeting people, this would be the wrong rig to drive. Often when we park, it's like the circus pulled into town. In

"If you don't like meeting people, this would be the wrong rig to drive."

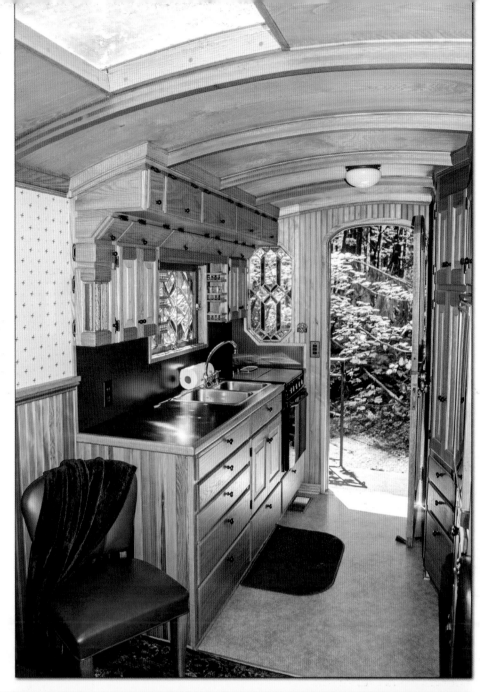

More...

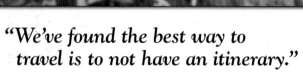

"We've found the best way to travel is to not have an itinerary."

37 years of use, we have never had anything but positive interactions from the people we've met. (Lloyd, this is not entirely the truth. In the redwoods, a few years ago, we encountered a campground manager who really didn't like "buses", but one person in 37 years certainly qualifies as an anomaly.)

We've found the best way to travel is to not have an itinerary. Be willing to stop wherever it looks good. Waking up in the morning, and looking out through the windows at something new, is a joyous experience. You can't own all of the beautiful places in the world, but you can have many of them for a few days for little or nothing. *Note:* Does not include Wal-Mart parking lots.

Should you build a house truck? Certainly. Don't be afraid to copy ideas, or blend different structures and styles together. Carpentry is an extremely old profession, and practically everything has already been done once in some form, or another.

Copying other styles is merely a way for carrying on the traditions of carpentry; another journeyman once told me "You steal with your eyes." I have been a union carpenter working in the Portland area for 37 years, and I think the independence of thought shown in the Shelter publications and by its contributors demonstrates that carpentry is still a living art form.

 www.federalhousetruck.com

"*...carpentry is still a living art form.*"

Rob's French Army House Truck

Rob Mason

Hello Lloyd/People of Shelter Pubs,

My name's Rob Mason, I'm an artist living on Dartmoor, England. I've had an uncontrollable urge to build a house truck ever since a friend bought me a copy of *Home Work* about 5 years ago.

I'm looking for land to start a micro holding — and a shack on a truck seemed the perfect thing to provide shelter, avoid planning permission, and be mobile.

Here are some pictures of my recently completed project. It's a 1959 French army truck — a Simca Unic Marmon Bocquet (or SUMB).

The shack is built with wood from local sawmills, reclaimed bits, corrugated steel, and insulated with sheep wool. Friends Jo House and Charlie Goodvibes helped with the building, which only took about 3 weeks. I hadn't built anything like it before, but now I feel ready to build anything, albeit in a slightly wonky fashion.

I'm thinking of building a pickup truck camper van to tour Europe in next, followed by a new art studio on a hay bale trailer.

I'm hoping to take the truck for a few trips before I find a suitable plot for veggies and animals, and we have been talking about building another similar truck to sell.

Thanks for the life-changing inspiration, keep the books coming!

–Rob

 www.RobMasonArt.com

"It's a 1959 French army truck..."

MARMON COLOR SCHEME.

"I hadn't built anything like it before, but now I feel ready to build anything..."

"The shack is built with wood from local sawmills, reclaimed bits, corrugated steel, and insulated with sheep wool."

The Beermoth
Walter Micklethwait

Beermoth *(from Urban Dictionary):*

Someone, usually an alcoholic, who goes around trying to grab unattended and unfinished drinks in a bar or other drinking premises.

Behemoth *(from Wikipedia):*

A mythological beast mentioned in the book of Job. Metaphorically the name has come to be used for any extremely large or powerful entity.

THE BEERMOTH, SO CALLED for its extreme size and prodigious thirst, was one of those ideas that wouldn't go away. It's a 1954 Commer Q4, a hose-carrying truck. Hundreds of them were mothballed during the cold war as reserve stock for the Auxiliary Fire Service (UK), then sold off in the late 1980s for a matter of a few hundred pounds. Many of them were turned into travelers' trucks.

This was the fourth I looked at over a five-year period; the first was really rusty and needed a whole new back body, the second had a steel workshop body but had been fully hippied and had stained glass everywhere. Then this one turned up in a museum on the south coast of England with 4,800 miles on the clock, in immaculate, totally standard condition, and priced at $4,500. It took four days and a further $1,000 in gas to drive it the 650 miles back to the Scottish highlands.

We run the Inshriach estate in the Cairngorms National Park, and I had built a yurt back in 2010 to use as holiday accommodation. The Commer was the closest thing I could think of to a yurt on wheels, inspired by the trucks in *Home Work* and Roger Beck's book, *Some Turtles Have Nice Shells*. I raised the hood frame by 12″ for a bit more headroom and had a custom canvas made up with windows and roller curtains and French laces to open up certain sections.

It has a parquet floor partly salvaged from a Tudor mansion, a Victorian bed at the front, and for the time being, a 1950s Rayburn range (which is actually a bit heavy for it). I do my best to keep it road-legal.

One day I'm going on a very slow holiday around the west coast of Scotland, but for the time being it earns its keep being parked up with a view of the mountains and renting to holidaymakers, and it's carved out a bit of a niche for itself in the press and on TV.

www.inshriachhouse.com

"The Commer was the closest thing I could think of to a yurt on wheels, inspired by the trucks in Home Work *and Roger Beck's book,* Some Turtles Have Nice Shells.*"*

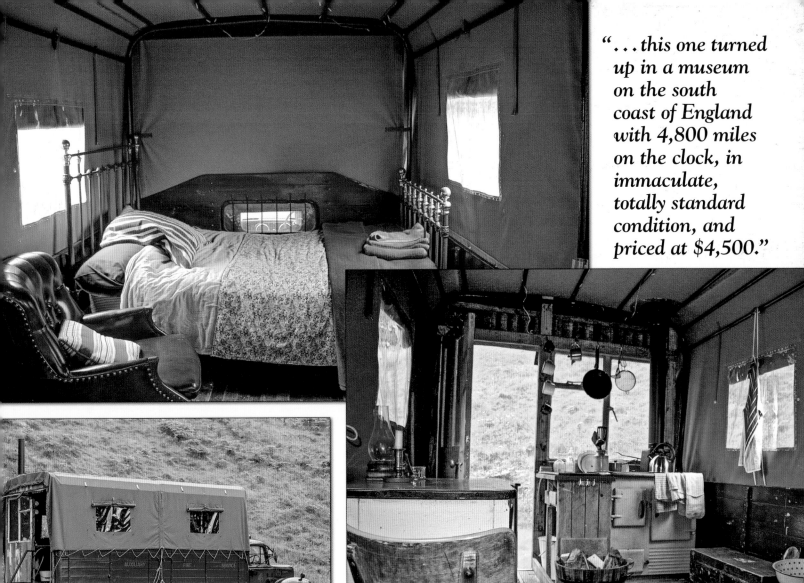

"...this one turned up in a museum on the south coast of England with 4,800 miles on the clock, in immaculate, totally standard condition, and priced at $4,500."

"I...had a custom canvas made up with windows and roller curtains and French laces to open up certain sections."

Shachagra

Family of Five Travels Through Europe and Turkey in Handmade 36′ RV

Doug Cuthbert

SHACHAGRA WAS BUILT BY, AND FOR A family of five with plans to travel for a year through Europe and Asia. A specific truck for a specific trip, she was a means to an end, not an end herself. Regardless, in the end she was pretty nice, and the trip was amazing.

From previous family travel, my wife Stef and I knew that sane, continuous travel for a year with two teens and a "tween" (Shannon 17, Charles 15, and Grace 11 (ShaChaGra)) would benefit from any stability and privacy we could offer the children.

We decided on an RV, but could find none that suited both our needs and wallet, so we designed and built our own. The 18 months of designing in my spare time and four months of building full time were well rewarded by the 16 months of comfortable travel and countless memories she provided.

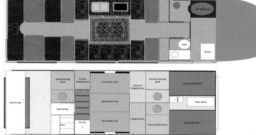

> "The name is not a Zen meditation technique or anything so deep, it's the first 3 letters of each child's name: Shannon, Charles, and Grace."

Galley and dinette occupy an open area 17 feet long and 8 feet wide, with windows on three sides.

The challenge of squeezing four staterooms into the truck was solved by hiding three of them in the kitchen cabinets and under the floor. The parents' room is the entire forward section of the body, to include the over-cab. The children's beds, sinks, and desks are under the "main deck" while the closets and three dressing areas are provided over 7 feet of headroom, and are hidden in and accessed through the galley cabinets.

A model I made helps to clarify the staterooms: Two of the beds are in the front just behind the cab. (The front is the shortest part.) You can see that they run fore and aft above the chassis rails.

Each room, entered from the galley, has a bed, closet, standing area 3′×3′, and a sink; everything is under the main floor except where you stand.

"I look back and I, too, am amazed that we got it done in basically four months!"

Built on an International 7500 4×6 chassis, standing 12½ feet tall, 8 feet wide and 33 feet long, Shachagra weighs in at 34,000 pounds, carries enough diesel for a 2,000-mile trek, and over 400 gallons of water (including the soaking tub and hot water heater). Powered by solar electric and diesel fuel, you'll only see her in an RV park if we want to use the pool!

Rustic Campers

Bill and Beck Goddard

Interior photos by Stella Mason

We converted our first van (a 1979 Leyland FG) into a home in 2007. It was a full restoration job and took a lot of hard work, but at the end of it we owned our very first home. After a happy three years living in the Welsh hills we began to get itchy feet, and although we moved around in the summer months, winters were always a stationary time.

For this adventure we needed something newer, so we converted our current home: a Mercedes Sprinter Luton. We packed up our belongings and, with dog at heel, took a boat to Spain. We traveled the coast living on the beaches and losing ourselves in the Picos Mountains, then wound our way down to Portugal — working along the way at small holdings and yoga retreats — meeting wild and wonderful people at every stop.

In the mountains of mid-Portugal we made some great friends and we built some round wood eucalyptus structures for them — a cabin frame, compost toilet, and lean-to.

We traveled down to southern Spain and over the Gibraltar Straits to the crazy souks and wild mountains of Morocco. From the blue city of Chefchouen we ventured south all the way to the edge of the Sahara Desert.

After an eight-month trip we returned home to set up Rustic Campers, a camper van conversion business. Whilst working as a tree surgeon and woodsman, I enjoy doing something more creative alongside; Beck works with textiles, her upholstery and fabrics compliment the wooden interiors of the vans beautifully. We live and work in the countryside, and our lifestyles mean that we spend the majority of our time outside; therefore nature has a very direct influence on what we do. We like to

"...we converted our current home: a Mercedes Sprinter Luton."

retain as much of the woods' natural beauty and shape as often as possible.

Doing something that we are passionate about and that suits our lifestyle is great. I love the idea of people living like this; less money, less stress, the opportunity to live closer to nature and the possibility of adventure at any time. We will live like this for some time to come and have the Shelter Publications books to thank for so much of our inspiration, to which we are forever indebted.

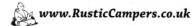 *www.RusticCampers.co.uk*

"I love the idea of people living like this; less money, less stress, the opportunity to live closer to nature and the possibility of adventure at any time."

50

"We live and work in the countryside, and our lifestyles mean that we spend the majority of our time outside."

"We traveled down to southern Spain and over the Gibraltar Straits to the crazy souks and wild mountains of Morocco."

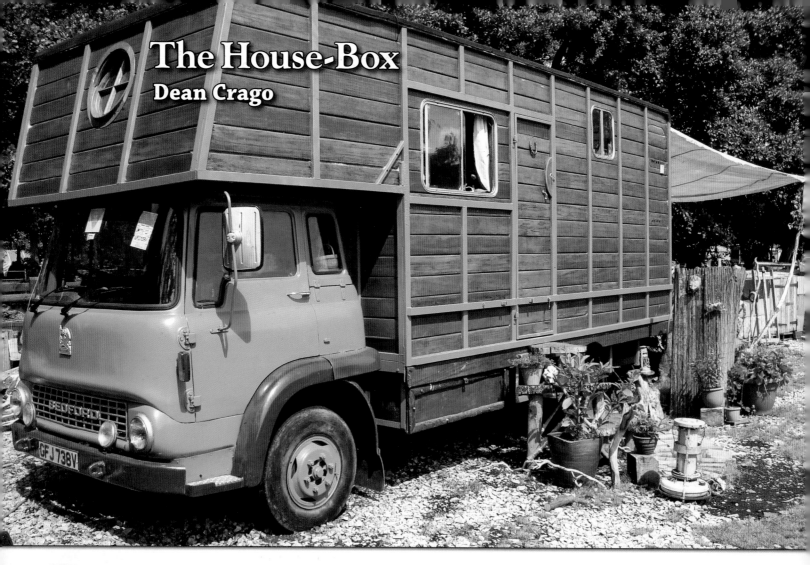

The House-Box
Dean Crago

THERE IS A COMMON MISCONCEPTION IN THE UK ABOUT living in a vehicle. Perceptions are polarized between spending up to £100,000 on ghastly "off-the-shelf" white fibreglass monstrosities, and squatting in the back of a cold, dark and damp old Ford transit with nothing but mosquitoes and rust for company.

In the past, my own living arrangements have swung like a pendulum between "free living" (squatting old arts warehouses and living in old buses in lay-bys) and at the other end, spending every penny I could scrape together on renting more traditional bricks 'n mortar houses. Neither had ever sat 100% comfortably with me (hence always swinging between the two).

Three years ago, my partner and I were living in a shared house in Glastonbury, Somerset UK. It was a beautiful home, surrounded by friends, and relatively cheap by comparison to what others were paying. However, we were both working full-time jobs (which neither of us really enjoyed) and come end of the month, after paying bills, we were left with hardly any money at all. It became clear to us that we didn't want to live like this forever. The result is "House-Box" (a play on "horse-box" coined by our old landlady Penny).

The idea was that through hard work, diligent research and thoughtful, conscious design, we could build a sustainable, affordable home in which to live, but without compromising the luxuries afforded by modern day living.

Our home, completely designed, restored and converted by ourselves, is a 7.5-ton 1979 Bedford TK. To the naked eye it looks like a traditional tweedy handmade home, but scratch the surface and there's enough sustainable technology to enable us to reduce our combined monthly outgoings from £800 (when we lived in our last "house") to just £20 on LPG!

We have a comprehensive PV solar set up, powering a 450-amp-hour bank of AGM batteries, on which we run just about anything we want (via a 1,500-watt pure sine wave inverter and reams and reams of ultra-low energy SMD LED "warm" lighting), a rainwater harvesting system that uses a process of five filters (including sediment, active charcoal, and UV filters) to provide all our water for drinking and washing, a composting toilet, hot shower, full range cooker, fridge, laptops, wood burning stove...the list goes on.

Since making the transition, we've never looked back. Not only is it an amazing and affordable way to live, but it's incredibly empowering being responsible for your own resources, rather than slaving away at a job you hate to pay some horrible multinational company to create nuclear waste to power your lights, or to flush your shit into the sea, only to see it again when surfing at high tide!

I loved the whole design and building process so much, and got such a great response from people who saw our work, that I jacked in my job and started my business "House-Box." Now I get to do what I love most for a living, and in the process am helping people to live the life that they dream of, too. In less than a year I already have a 9-month waiting list for conversions. I've recently finished my first large full conversion project as a professional (1989 7.5-ton Leyland roadrunner Horse-Box) It's for a couple of aerial acrobats who are on a worldwide tour with the "Batman Live" show, and I've almost finished a 3.5-ton box-van conversion for another circus performer (whose only design criteria was "room to do the splits and space for a 4 ft. snake tank!").

I'm in my element. I'm able to be creative for a living; one day I'm a carpenter, the next, plumber, the next, electrician.

It makes me laugh. My mum used to joke about when I was a kid, I would change my mind every day about what I wanted to do for a living as an adult. Now, as an adult, I get to do something different every day for a living!

Keep on keeping it real!

> "I'm in my element. I'm able to be creative for a living; one day I'm a carpenter, the next, plumber, the next, electrician."

Gas bottle burner

Tech specs:

- 360 AH battery capacity (AGM)
- 160w (2 × 80w) PV solar panels
- Heavy duty vehicle split charge system
- Steca PR3030 charge controller
- Blue Sea 12-way 12v fuse box
- 1,500w pure sine wave inverter
- SMD LED lighting throughout
- 1,050w sound system with multiple input points
- (300w amp and crossover for tops and mids/750w bass amp with "scoop" style bass bins built into seating area)
- Three-way fridge with freezer box (powered by LPG/12v or 240v)
- 120-litre water tank (with baffles and external lockable filler cap)
- Shurflo 13-lpm 12v automatic pressure-switched pump

- Homemade micro-guttering throughout with "first flush" system
- 8-micron 10″ sediment filter
- 4-micron 10″ activated carbon filter
- Inline UV water filter
- Carver Cascade 2 water heater
- Hot shower and hot/cold kitchen taps
- Compost collecting toilet with urine separation
- Ultra-low power computer fans for collection area door

Solar control center

www.house-box.co.uk
dean@house-box.co.uk

Traveller Dave

Dave Fawcett

1966 Leyland Albion "Chieftain" CH3a Albion EN335 4-cylinder 5.5 litre. 98 hp. diesel 6-speed box

"...it's functional with what for many folks are very basic facilities. But a bed, burner, cookers enough!"

L IVING IN A 1966 ALBION Chieftain lorry, converted to a home, Traveller Dave has spent much of the past two decades in Europe, working on farms and travelling around, all the time taking photographs of the other interesting traveller homes he has seen from mid-1980s Glastonbury to France and Portugal. All manner of vehicles are shown here, creatively converted to full-time homes.

Making their homes from redundant buses and lorries, travellers have made a fantastic variety of one-off mobile homes using their own creativity and materials they have recycled or restored, and Traveller Dave has managed to photograph and document these colorful vehicles from the early 1980s onwards.

The adoption by those of us known by many names but commonly referred to as the "New Travellers" of buses and coaches retired from PSV service arose from the emergence of the commercial and free festival scene in the late '60s and its development during the '70s.

This led to many deciding to follow an itinerant lifestyle,

at least during the summer months, which meant that various types of transport were adopted, including horse-drawn wagons, small vans and ex-passenger service vehicles. The latter had also been commonly adapted for mobile accommodation by the UK's fairground families in the 1950s and 1960s and were often available cheaply, either direct from coach and bus firms, or via auctions, specialized dealers and scrapyards.

Interior arrangements were often basic to start with; most of the original seats having been removed, a platform for the bed was often built across the rear end, a wood burner installed and a rudimentary kitchen fitted. Further refinements depended on the owner's needs, family size, skills, and what could be found in industrial skips!

The same applies to the exterior appearance, often initially left in the previous owner's colour scheme, but also often repainted with flamboyant colours or with an artistic landscape scene, for example, by some of the talented mobile artists to

be found within the travelling community.

Structural alterations could mean anything from the panelling over of some or all of the side windows, to creating open rear platforms (or top decks) or the addition of a second-level bedroom by attaching a small van body to the roof!

As well as providing transport for the owner(s) and their children, many homes were also used to transport various domestic animals, often just cats and dogs for company, but also goats, hens, ducks, geese and sometimes horses.

 **www.TravellerDave.co.uk**

This is the "summer" look as in the winter a heavy door curtain helps keep draughts at bay and a woven rug covers the planks as far as the Singer treadle sewing machine, which doubles as a table, on the left side.

By now things had been well-organized for several years; it's functional with what for many folks are very basic facilities — a bed, burner, and cookers — enough! Many visitors at Vintage Expos ask why there's no shower unit...but never dare ask where I've hidden a chemical toilet! What's wrong with a spade?

More...

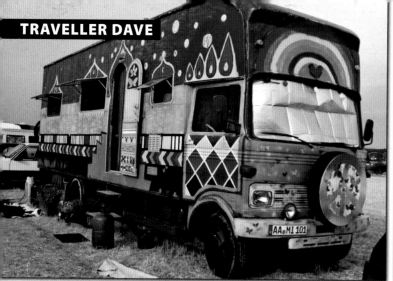

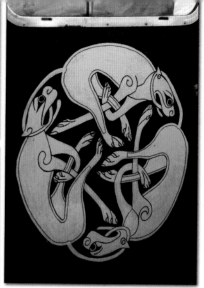

teeny tiny LIVING

oPhelia Kwong & Julien Lafaille

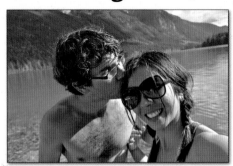

WE ARE A COUPLE (and a tiny dog) living in the rainforest of British Columbia. Our love of being in nature, climbing rocks, and riding bikes inspired us to move away from the city. The desire to live a simpler, less cluttered life led us to rent a cabin in the woods. After a year of living in the mountains and by the ocean, we knew that country life was for us and we decided to become homeowners.

"…we were not interested in spending our lives working to pay the mortgage until the end of time."

It was at this point that we were struck by the housing prices in one of the most expensive real estate areas of the world (near Whistler, BC, Canada). We were not interested in a house in the suburbs or a condo in town. We wanted to continue living in the forest, but the land that was available for sale was often remote, without water/electricity and treed (*i.e.*, no road/clearing for building a house), not to mention being overpriced (in our opinion). Even though we could afford it, we were not interested in spending our lives working to pay the mortgage until the end of time.

So we began to explore creative ways to have our very own home despite the economic realities. We sought ideas through conversations, the Internet and books (including *Tiny Homes*!) And that is how this project came to be.

Instead of locking ourselves into a long-term loan, we decided to start with building a home, paying it off and then eventually buying land when we know exactly where we want to be. When that time comes, we will pack our stuff and be able to move our home because it is a house on wheels! For now, we are renting land on a farm with animals along the river. Soon we will pay off the cost of the bus project, and since our land rent is a quarter of our city apartment rent, it allows us plenty of time and money to do the things we love! ☺

TeenyTinyLiving.blogspot.com

"For now, we are renting land on a farm with animals along the river."

Vital Statistics

Bus: *76-passenger 1991 International school bus (diesel)*

Electricity: *Hooked up to a 200-amp service. All plugs are 110V, except for washer/dryer, which are 240V.*

Plumbing: *Water comes from a well and is brought into the bus for the shower, washer and kitchen faucet. Water pipes are insulated with heat tape and foam.*

Propane: *Powers the gas range and water heater*

Water heater: *On-demand propane water heater that is attached to the exterior of the bus*

Heating: *Two 2 KW electric baseboard heaters*

Insulation: *Flooring and walls: plastic moisture barrier and foam*

Ceiling: *Original fiberglass insulation*

Toilet: *Composting toilet*

Appliances: *Gas range, refrigerator, washer, dryer*

"Our love of being in nature, climbing rocks, and riding bikes inspired us to move away from the city."

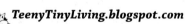

"... since our land rent is a quarter of our city apartment rent, it allows us plenty of time and money to do the things we love!"

School Bus Medicine Show Gypsy Wagon

Doug Young

I FOUND THE SCHOOL BUS (1946 Chevrolet) in a junkyard in the early 1970's...took me three days to decide to buy it...offered too much...drove it to a mechanic's on two cylinders...he rebuilt the engine while I worked on the wiring.

It is 25′, bumper to bumper, parks in a normal parking space...the interior is 16′ from driver's seat to back door. It had been gutted of all seats, had a wooden kitchen chair for a driver's seat and a plywood board stretched across the back door for a bed. It had been used as a fishing shack.

After driving around Colorado, including most mountain passes...Berthoud Pass was interesting...I decided on a simple floor plan and began the reconstruction.

I removed the old roof and temporarily skinned it with heavyweight gold canvas, did more passes and a trip to St. Louis delivering sculpture on what became known as the "Grandmother" trip...mine lived in Jefferson City, MO, my accomplice's in St. Louis.

I then began welding the new roof by raising the four existing roof ribs 12″ and fabricating the back, skinning it with the outer and inner sheet metal panels, and scrounging for the rest. The center vista cruise window over the cab was a back hatch out of some scrapped vehicle... fit fine...no glass, used Lexan which has fogged over the years...the two side arcs came from the back window's inner sheet metal, again fitting just right.

I drove it to Corpus Christi, Texas and lived out of it while working there. I wrote a song while living between the Naval Air Station and the biker bars called "Flower Bluff Blues"... the intro is: "Something in my solar plexus wants to get me out of Texas."

The interior is fully insulated and finished with aspen bead board trimmed with redwood, with stainless steel behind the wood stove from a catering truck or roach coach. The skylight is the old rear exit door window, and the new rear door came from the T-Spoon Ranch outside of Guffey, CO.

I've lived in the bus several times over the years while caretaking ranches; the longest stint was a year and a half. I'd like to put a rear deck on it this summer...a platform for musical events and theatrical perfomances and snake oil shows...

I need to do exterior bodywork and paint...keeping in the gypsy or circus wagon motif, and would love to find a diesel engine for a multi-fuel conversion. If it comes down to it, I'll hook a single tree to the front and pull it with mules to keep it rolling.

And yes, I'm back living in the bus again with a cat named Hopper.

"You're either on the bus or off!" said my old grade school bus driver.

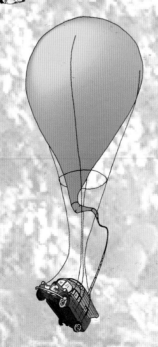

www.shltr.net/thom-young

"I've lived in the bus several times over the years while caretaking ranches; the longest stint was a year and a half."

VAL·616
COLORADO

"'You're either on the bus or off!' said my old grade school bus driver."

"Something in my solar plexus wants to get me out of Texas."

From House to School Bus Home
Jim Bob & Candice Salazar

"...a comfortable, paid-for, mobile house that is custom-made to suit our family of four."

WE CONVERTED OUR 1989, 76-passenger school bus into an alternative living situation to solve the predicament in which we found ourselves.

We desperately wanted off the bureaucratic treadmill and to get into a simple life: to raise our kids ourselves, make art, grow our own food, and enjoy each other.

By selling our traditional house, becoming debt-free and converting our bus into a house on wheels, we were able to have a comfortable, paid-for, mobile house that is custom-made to suit our family of four.

Our school bus conversion is just the beginning of our journey. We are grateful for its hospitality and looking forward to our adventures together.

Zeb and Lena Marie

 AdventuresOfTheYellowSchoolBus.blogspot.com

Shot from front of bus, looking toward back

Shot from back of bus, looking toward front

All dishes are on shelf above sink.

King-size bed

Stock tank bathtub

Toys, books, clothes stored underneath bed. We couldn't function in such a small space without this area.

"Our school bus conversion is just the beginning of our journey."

Vital Statistics

Propane tank: 100 lb. cylinder

Water tank: We are hooked up to the water in the RV park. Once we get to our piece of property, we will use 15k-gallon rainwater storage tanks.

Water heater: Takagi T-K JR2/OS-LP It is bolted to the outside of the bus. It comes with a little heater that keeps it from freezing up on cold, cold days.

Wiring: All 110 wiring

Plumbing: Waterlines are done with ½″ Pex tubing, waste lines are done with 1½″ PVC pipe.

Gas lines: ½″ black pipe

Heating: We are using a propane Kozy-World 20k BTU blue flame heater for the whole bus.

Insulation: Not much, the floors have ½″ Dow foam insulation with a layer of tarpaper in between, the walls and ceiling have whatever was manufactured with the bus.

Appliances: We have a full-size fridge, stove, front-loading washer — all Kenmore bought at Sears.

Flooring: 4′ × 8′ × ¾″ birch plywood, washed with latex paint and 4 coats of poly

Bus: 38 ft. long × 7.5 ft. wide × 6.5 tall, 76-passenger, 1989 GMC chassis with a Ward body, 13 windows, Cummins diesel with an Allison automatic transmission

Bed: King-size

Air conditioning: Two 10k BTU window units

Jif's Bus

Richard Ieian Jones

Hi Lloyd,

Visited my friend Jif (Ian Jeffries) the other day. He is a "Zen" Welder. I have never met anybody with such an understanding of metal. It's like his mind gets inside it in its molten or crystalline state?

I have known him for years. He's the one responsible for guiding me off the straight dull road and showing me a different reality. He is also famed as a "freegan" or skip diver as we used to call it. That's skanking the out-of-date food that gets abandoned by the supermarket because it"s past its sell-by date. Still perfectly edible as we know. There was a film crew made a documentary with him in it a few years back.

I thought you might be interested in his home: a 1950s Bristol "lowdecker" double-decker bus.

It has been a traveler vehicle for a number of years and Jif's home for about the past 10 or 12 years. Before Jif got it, it changed hands regularly between a pair of friends, as one needed the money or went off traveling. Then one year it was heading for Glastonbury Festival and disaster struck. It was sat in traffic at the back of a motorway tailback, and the lorry behind didn't notice it had stopped. It shunted right up the back of it, writing it off. The back lower deck was cut off. Jif acquired it a short while later in a sorry state. He has spent years slowly rebuilding, customizing, and fitting it out.

The back of the bus got reworked into a small workshop, and a Gucci hydraulic ramp was fitted from a dead horse box. So Jif could ride his motorbike right up inside and hit the road. It's an amazing piece of engineering. You turn a knob and *shhhhhhhhh*, the ramp descends, and top opens. Just needs some dry ice and lasers.

Inside, most of the top deck has been cut out, leaving a room at each end (one for Jif and one for his son Freddy) and a walkway down one side connecting the two. An old Rayburn range supplies heating and hot running water. The plumbing is pretty funky, but hey, hot and cold water on tap, can't be bad.

He is now doing a bit more of a refit. Workshop has gone, and living space extended, kennel for the dog at the back. Ash ceiling, and sink drainer, all homemade. The sliding silver mesh cupboard doors are filters from some air-handling unit, cut down to fit; the channel they run in is a plastic curtain rail he attacked with a grinder to make slots for the doors.

He now has a nice set of velvet curtains courtesy of an ex-girlfriend's mum. He hand-made every curtain ring on lathe, hundreds of 'em!

> *"Inside, most of the top deck has been cut out, leaving a room at each end (one for Jif and one for his son Freddy) and a walkway down one side connecting the two."*

"It has been a traveler vehicle for
a number of years and Jif's home
for about the past 10 or 12 years."

The Wayland Family School Bus

Cody and Lindsey Wayland

> "We had this really big awakening after we spent so much money renting a home…"

> "We had a strong pull to move forward, brave and radical, by making our life from scratch."

THE BUS IS A 1988 FORD; IT NOW stands 13 feet tall by 25 feet long. There is a very small wall clock hanging on the back window frame—a pocket watch from Cody's family dating back more than a hundred years—illustrating that all we have is time and that time is always now. The planer tool was invaluable in this project, planing thousands of recycled dump redwood boards into the walls and floorboards and cabinets and drawers and shelves and doors of our tiny home.

The wood in the interior of the bus is eight parts California redwood to two parts Texas Pecan hardwood; my dad drove the pecan from Texas, where he got it decades ago secondhand. The bus juxtaposes modern and old fashioned in many facets: the metal and the wood, the tankless hot water heater

and a water pitcher pump, the potential to cover miles somewhat quickly, and the potential to quickly settle into a nesting place. The ideas behind the bus are deep-rooted dreams for me, and my husband's creative building and aesthetic sensibilities brought the dreams to fruition.

There is a refurbished 1894 Senator wood stove, which sits on the wheel well and acts as a centerpiece for our home, both for heat and cooking (the Senator cost $200 more than the bus in its original state!).

We had this really big awakening after we spent so much money renting a home when—at the end of our stint there—we had nothing to show for all that money. For us, it was time to put our money where our thoughts were—outside the mortgage. We had a strong pull to move forward, brave and radical, by making our life from scratch.

"Until one is committed, there is hesitancy, the chance to draw back, always ineffectiveness. Concerning all acts of initiative (and creation), there is one elementary truth the ignorance of which kills countless ideas and splendid plans: that the moment one definitely commits oneself, then Providence moves too. All sorts of things occur to help one that would never otherwise have occurred. A whole stream of events issues from the decision, raising in one's favor all manner of unforeseen incidents and meetings and material assistance, which no man could have dreamed would have come his way. Whatever you can do, or dream you can do, begin it. Boldness has genius, power, and magic in it. Begin it now."

–Johann Wolfgang von Goethe, 1749–1832

 **www.GlitterAndGritGirl.com**

> "The bus juxtaposes modern and old fashioned in many facets…"

"...the potential to cover miles somewhat quickly, and the potential to quickly settle into a nesting place."

"The planer tool was invaluable in this project, planing thousands of recycled dump redwood boards..."

Steve and Katy's School Bus Home

Katy Erickson

STEVE AND I LIVED IN our converted school bus full time from December 2009 to October 2011. Then temptation struck: I got a job that included a staff house overlooking the Wenatchee River. We took this more conventional living arrangement, and I'm sure everyone thought we'd finally gotten over our bus phase. They were wrong.

The longer we lived in the house, the more things we missed about the bus. We couldn't watch snow or rain or sunflowers out of 13 windows at once or clean up in 10 minutes or have friends over for bus parties. Even worse, I was giving up precious hours of life in exchange for extra rooms we didn't need.

The bus had everything: a stove-top and oven, a five-gallon hot water tank, a fridge, a wood stove, and plenty of space in which to live, sleep, and eat. Even "deprivations" like using a composting toilet, taking sponge baths, and making do with less square footage had given us the satisfaction of knowing that we were saving resources.

So, in August 2013, we moved back into our bus. Steve added custom touches like live edge trim and shelving, a tiled hearth, refinished bamboo floors, hidden LED strip lighting and a 75-percent-efficient wood stove with a cook plate. Our hosts, Dan and Lois Oberg, were happy to have us back. We help them with house and garden projects in exchange for space to park the bus and grow food. This mutually beneficial communal living is perhaps the best part of bus life.

If you'd like to find out more about what it's really like to live in a school bus, you can follow us on our blog.

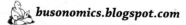 *busonomics.blogspot.com*

"The bus had everything: a stove-top and oven, a five-gallon hot water tank, a fridge, a wood stove, and plenty of space in which to live, sleep, and eat."

"...using a composting toilet, taking sponge baths, and making do with less square footage had given us the satisfaction of knowing that we were saving resources."

The School Bus Experience

Lucas Sweeten

MY FIRST ROLLING HOME was built for discovery. I was the driver, but not always. Even behind the wheel it seemed I was just along for the ride. "Where to next?" "Mexico... The Yukon maybe... Alaska?"

Attached to the rear of the bus was a horse trailer. Inside, my best friend and I would filter waste vegetable oil into 55-gallon drums; also inside was a chopped '74 Honda CB750 motorcycle. Vegetable oil made everything inside and everyone glisten.

A canoe was mounted on top of the bus. We housed bicycles inside. No terrain seemed unmanageable and no idea unobtainable.

Adventure was at every turn; new friends at every stop. There was a lifetime of experience rolled up into an 8 ft. by 40 ft. hollow metal tube.

My second bus (shown here) is becoming a home. A place to house all past experience. A place to welcome new experience, new innovations and inspire passersby. A place to inspire myself.

There's no manual or rules for living in or building a bus. It's free from perfection, ruled by creative imagination only. I don't think of it as a bus or a home really; it's more of an experience. You create it, and well, to a certain extent, it helps create you.

Photo: MGDR/Whitney Sacksteder

"I don't think of it as a bus or a home really; it's more of an experience."

*"'Where to next?' 'Mexico...
The Yukon maybe... Alaska?'"*

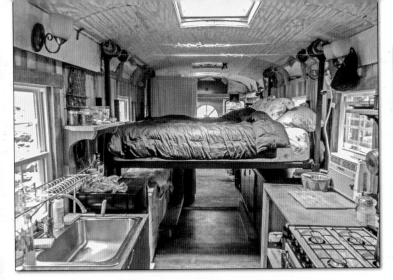

"Adventure was at every turn; new friends at every stop."

Photo: MGDR/Whitney Sacksteder

School Bus Dentist

by Dr. Peter Walford
Photos by Michael McNamara

I MOVED ONTO A SAILBOAT IN Vancouver in 1975, wounded from divorce, looking for something small enough to manage. I ended up in the midst of the eccentric and somewhat scruffy boatbuilding/offshore maritime tribe of the day, and took to it like a duck to water. I ended up seeing most of the west coast by sail over the next five years, including places I didn't get to by road for another 30 years.

This left me with a love for islands, islanders, and small spaces. Eventually the trail reconnected me with my profession as a dentist in a new way. While between boats I converted a school bus — the biggest I could find — 38 feet — into a two-chair dental clinic. I did it part-time, just a few days a month, for several years. By then I had a patient following, and I cut the tie with conventional society and made it my only livelihood, serving Hornby and Denman islands north of Vancouver.

After 17 years that bus rusted out, and during its last four dying years I committed 3,000 hours working to replace it with the ultimate mobile dental clinic.

The new bus, finished in 2003, is a 38-foot Bluebird, propane-powered, and has in-floor hot-water heat, three-zone music, digital x-rays and a state-of-the-art clinic — all in gulf island chic — thanks to the collaboration of the many woodworkers and artisans of these islands. I got some great new woodworking tools and a whole lot of creative joy out of the adventure, and have been able to live in clean air and beautiful surroundings, being the dental custodian for these very wonderful islanders.

I've ridden my bike home from work through woods and alongside the ocean for 27 years now. At 66, a happy marriage, four kids, 6 grandkids, and a big organic garden later, it proves to me that you are not wrong for following the things you love.

P.S.: I took the creative energy released in the bus buildup to start making dental inventions and become a recognized innovator in my field. I've never stopped since. Now I'm making pretty good money at that. Once you discover you can actually make things with your own hands, it just becomes a question of how you are going to apply it.

> *"I converted a school bus — the biggest I could find — 38 feet — into a two-chair dental clinic."*

> *"The new bus, finished in 2003, is a 38-foot Bluebird, propane-powered, and has in-floor hot-water heat, three-zone music, digital x-rays and a state-of-the-art clinic."*

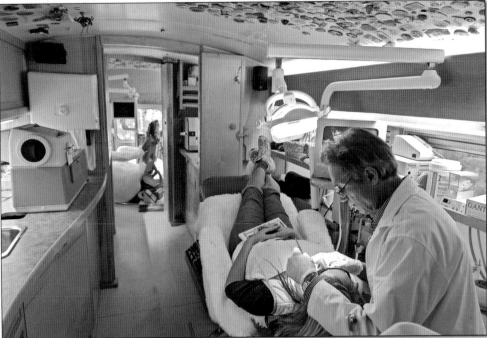

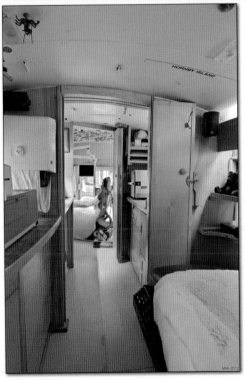

"I've ridden my bike home from work through woods and alongside the ocean for 27 years now."

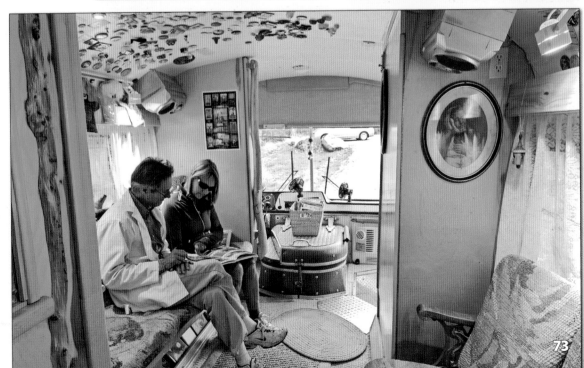

Homemade Vardo
Paul and Melissa Rodgers

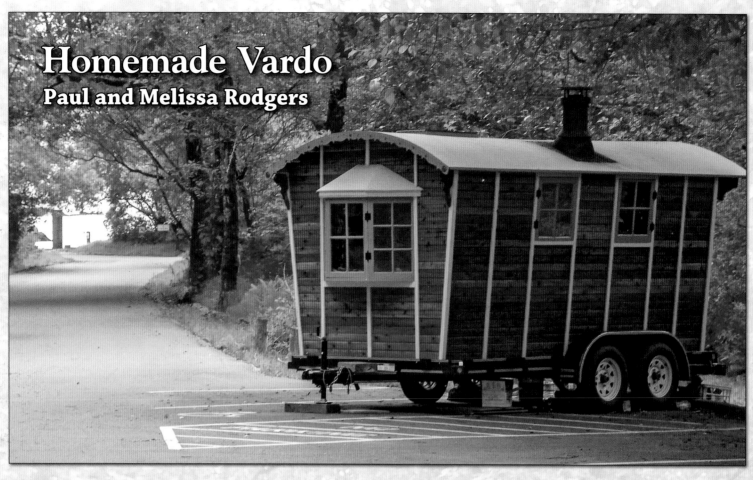

Photos by Cliff Volpe

IT ALL STARTED WITH A SINK — A HAND-HAMMERED copper sink from Mexico — so inspiring that we built the gypsy wagon around it. An old-style, horse-drawn *vardo* wasn't practical for our needs, so we opted to construct a newer version on a 14′ × 7′ car hauler.

It had to have traditional elements though, like slanted walls, a bowed roof and exterior framing. We knew it needed to be lightweight and strong — and we wanted it to be ever so slightly gaudy.

The walls are ¹¹⁄₁₆″ tongue-and-groove cedar, which we stained and varnished. The roof is ⅜″ Douglas fir plywood, coated with an elastomeric paint to shed the rain. With an emphasis on using either natural or reclaimed materials, salvage yards and Craigslist were veritable gold mines — as were our own storage sheds and woodpile. A beautiful old piece of eastern black walnut made a perfect kitchen counter.

For maximum space versatility, the shelves and seats can be folded up and fastened out of the way, and the massive drawers and cupboards under the bed provide ample storage. We have no running water or electricity, but plenty of comfort and convenience with a propane cooktop, large bay window, and a skylight that lets us see the stars at night. Two of our favorite decorative features are the hand-cast bronze door-knocker and painting of Ganesha — both created by our son Max.

There's nothing quite like gathering with friends to play music and swap stories on a rainy night, fueled by our homemade cabernet, with warmth from the wood stove and light from the kerosene lanterns.

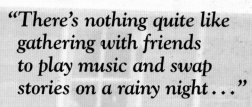

"An old-style, horse-drawn vardo wasn't practical for our needs, so we opted to construct a newer version on a 14′ × 7′ car hauler."

"There's nothing quite like gathering with friends to play music and swap stories on a rainy night . . ."

> "It's on a trailer and can be moved any time (at speeds up to 60 mph)."

The Don Vardo

Dee Williams

Photos by Karen Wolf

THIS 54-SQUARE-FOOT STRUCTURE WAS DESIGNED and built by Katy Anderson, working in conjunction with Portland Alternative Dwellings.

It's designed as a space to write, paint, hang out, hide out, get away, or as a place to host visiting guests for a few days at a time. It features a small kitchenette, a writing desk, and a pullout bed.

It's on a trailer and can be moved any time (at speeds up to 60 mph).

Katy's skillful and creative craftsmanship, and strategic and elegant integration of green building materials (salvaged, renewable, etc.) are inspirations to tiny house enthusiasts.

What you can't see in the photos: radiant heat flooring and rope lights along the interior eve that cast an upward glow at night, making the house look like it's parked above water.

The plans are available through *PADtinyhouses.com*, and are free to students and teachers.

 www.PADtinyhouses.com

"It's designed as a space to write, paint, hang out,
hide out, get away, or as a place to host visiting guests . . ."

The Reading Gypsy Wagon

Peter & Donna Thomas

IN 2010–11 WE TRAVELED around the country as "Wandering Book Artists" in our Gypsy Wagon Bookmobile. Our journey to becoming wandering book artists began in the 1970s, when, dressed like Robin Hood and Maid Marion, we taught papermaking and bookbinding at the Renaissance Pleasure Faires in California.

We also sold blank books and letterpress-printed broadsides from ramshackle booths we built from recycled lumber, swathed in burlap. When our daughters were born, we constructed a small gypsy wagon to use as our booth so they would have a refuge from the wild hubbub of the fair.

It was a colorful and charming vehicle that we always dreamed of taking on a road trip around the country, but pulling it was a white-knuckle adventure, as it shook and wobbled like a ship in a storm.

That wagon served us well for many years. In 2008, it burned in a wildfire, leaving us only a pile of melted metal and memories.

We cleaned up the wreckage, and then started building a new and more roadworthy trailer. We modeled it after a "Reading" wagon, one of the many styles of horse-drawn homes, or *vardos*, made for Romany travelers in England during the late 19th and early 20th centuries.

It was built with the assistance of Richard Raucina of Raucina Cabinets in Midpines, California. When people asked if we were going to pull it with a horse, we replied with a quick smile, "No, we're going to use a ram. A Dodge Ram."

Since no blueprints were available, we used pictures and our own elevation sketches as guides. It was constructed on a 16´ flatbed car-hauler trailer and measures 14´ long by 8´ tall and is 8´ at the widest point.

The exterior studs and siding are poplar, the roof is copper, the interior is sugar pine (cut and milled by Raucina), and the ceiling is Yosemite giant sequoia.

The exterior is painted with bright bold colors. It has heavy wrought-iron hardware, stained glass windows, flowers and birds carved into wooden corbels, with herald angels in place of gargoyles at each corner. Inside is a single open room with a propane heater, cook stove, sink, and retractable workbench / kitchen table. At the rear there is a curtained-off bed covered with a pile of patchwork quilts.

There were not many other gypsy wagons on the roads, so when our "Parnassus on Wheels" passed by, heads turned. People would chase us down to look inside and find out what we were doing.

When we told them we were book artists, we would usually get confused looks and so have to tell them more. We would say that book artists make books like painters make paintings, and that we make our own paper, hand draw or print the pages, bind the book, and then look for a buyer.

Peter would use the gypsy wagon as a metaphor for an artist's book, saying, "When you look inside a regular RV, what do you think? Usually nothing," or, "How practical." But when people see our gypsy wagon they get excited, curious, and something magical always happens. Commercially produced books are like regular RVs, practical and full of information. Artists' books are like our gypsy wagon: they inspire imagination and wonder, and share something of the artist who created them.

"It was constructed on a 16´ flatbed car-hauler trailer and measures 14´ long by 8´ tall and is 8´ at the widest point."

"The exterior studs and siding are poplar, the roof is copper, the interior is sugar pine . . ."

"We modeled it after a 'Reading' wagon, one of the many styles of horse-drawn homes, or vardos, made for Romany travelers in England during the late 19th and early 20th centuries."

"Inside is a single open room with a propane heater, cook stove, sink, and retractable workbench/ kitchen table."

Matt's Solar-Powered Wagon

Matt Hayman

ABOUT SEVEN YEARS AGO I LEFT HOME AND BOUGHT A camper van with a friend to drive across Europe. It got as far as Antwerp in Belgium before it blew up. With little remaining cash I bought an old Royal Mail van and flung some beds and a cooker inside, and our journey continued.

Within a year, I had rebuilt the interior on the side of the road three times, each interior more sophisticated than the last, and I was addicted. I traveled far and wide, everywhere from Bosnia to Wales.

My next home was bigger, with space above the cab for a bed; it was my grandest project yet, inspired in part by Lloyd's books. It even had a shower!

Then, whilst my partner Anna and I were traveling in the Middle East, we decided not to return to van life. With ever-rising fuel prices and a desire for a garden, some chickens, and more space, we had a vision of a yurt, a slower pace.

We sold the home on wheels and erected a yurt behind my father's house, overlooking some fields. Later came this wagon, for which all my vans were practice — I see that now. Life is a progression that never ends.

The wagon has no engine to maintain, no road tax or insurance — a breath of fresh air! It's five stars for us, with hot running water, 500 watts of solar power, wood-burning stoves, an oven, a hob (warming shelf on back end of wood stove) and grill. We also have a sawdust toilet inspired by Joe Jenkins, and we have a garden and chickens. Life is great.

The yurt structure can load inside the wagon and it can be towed, (by a vehicle we don't own!)

The yurt structure can load inside the wagon and it can be towed (by a vehicle we don't own! What are friends for, hey?). Having now been in one place and feeling relatively settled, I am comforted by the fact that our entire home, all 430 square feet of it, is fully portable. With no rush or desperation, we are open to expanding out of my father's place to live with some like-minded folks and spiral ever higher. I work as a craftsman and a handyman, and I have a website showcasing many of my creations.

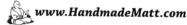 *www.HandmadeMatt.com*

"It's five stars for us, with hot running water, 500 watts of solar power, wood-burning stoves, an oven . . . and grill."

Gypsy Wagons by Joseph

Joseph Crowell

AS A 10-YEAR OLD KID watching *The Wizard of Oz*, I was really enchanted when Dorothy steps into the back of the snake oil salesman's vardo to gaze into his crystal ball. I was mesmerized by the beauty of that rig, and now, as an adult, I love building my own versions of these mobile cabins.

I worked with my dad. At age 13, he taught me how to use tools. In my early 20s, I ran into a man named Silverbear and helped him build his bus. I took that knowledge with me, and in 1985 built my own bus, with VW on top. I hit the road in it and did the Dead shows.

Later I met a man named Sunny Baba (nothing short of a pure artist) who built several rigs, all beautiful, all inspiring. He visited me in 2008 and triggered the Gypsy

wagon campaign that I am now pursuing. I am on my seventh project, and have sold all my previous wagons.

I use about 40–50% recycled wood, and scrounge almost daily in the Shakespeare Festival stage production dumpster, pulling out all types of useables. I currently live in a 1946 Spartan 23 ft. trailer on a farm outside Ashland, Oregon. Life is good.

I use a lot of recycled materials in the construction process, each wagon having its own unique array of found and bought items. The framing is 2″ × 2″ studs with 1.5″ rigid foam insulation in the walls and ceiling and ¾″ foam in

the floor, making my structures very strong and warm.

The roof has plenty of overhang clearance for weather protection, made from plywood and steel, and laminated with a strong plastic membrane. The 110 power uses #14 Romex, and #12 for the 12v power. My kitchens have a sink with a fresh water tank and pump, propane two-burner cook stove, and optional fridge.

Depending on the size of my campers, each has a good solid axle to carry the load

(although my trailers are made of wood, I use lightweight materials and the campers are surprisingly light).

The exterior wood finish is a high-grade spar varnish, the trim paint is exterior gloss latex, and the interior is water-based non-toxic polyurethane.

The interiors are my favorite parts of the creation process where I get to use natural woods, stained glass windows, found antique items, and curvy tree limbs, all adding to that hobbit-house feel. Enjoy the magic.

www.GypsyWagonsByJoseph.com

"...natural woods, stained glass windows, found antique items, and curvy tree limbs, all adding to that hobbit-house feel."

Willow's Wagon
Willow De La Roche

"...as an adult, I now realize that my dream is to live in the wilds, with other like-minded people..."

Photos by Amy Behrens Clark

THIS PROJECT SPRINGS from my love of nature and my desire to live as close as possible to it, but in a versatile way that allows me to move with the seasons whilst sampling different cultures and environments. My name is Willow De La Roche; I'm an artist and I was born in England in 1984.

When I was a child, I lived in an alternative way, and was home-educated. I was able to travel to and live in many places and communities all over the world. This led me to develop my own life philosophy without interference from state education. I was taught to believe in myself and that almost anything is possible if you put your mind to it.

I feel that being brought up in a nomadic way has given me insight into different people and their cultures; I have been able to develop my sense of self and what I believe in, which is individuality and living in a way that respects our environment.

After a "footloose and fancy free" childhood, I went to a Krishnamurti International School, then Dartington College of Arts; this meant a more conventional way of life for a while. But as an adult, I now realize that my dream is to live in the wilds, with other

like-minded people, in my own home that I can move wherever I wish.

These things are what inspired me to build my little home on wheels — which I could not have done without the help of my partner Milo, a skilled carpenter and sculptor. He shares a similar outlook to mine, in living closely to nature. He feels strongly about environmental matters and finding a creative way for sustained alternative living. He was also home-educated.

I have had great support throughout, from being lent most of the money for materials, to Milo giving so much of his time and the use of his workshop. My friends and family have also made key contributions, and I have been able to keep many of my original ideas for the design due to huge generosity from the lovely people in my life.

I started building in 2010 when I realized how much I wanted my own home. Most modern buildings are to me unnatural and stifling.

Another factor is that many of my generation are priced out of the housing market and forced to find other solutions.

In October 2011, I made some sketches, and after some drafts, I settled on a design and learned how to do scaled architectural drawings.

I bought a twin-axle flatbed trailer and we extended the floor width of the trailer, working within legal size restrictions.

We built a stud frame with

plywood on both sides, and insulation in between, and covered it with a waterproof membrane and sheathed it with cedar. The bow top is made of

corrugated iron and the floor of old pine floorboards, sanded and waxed.

Milo welded up a wood-burning stove from an old gas tank. All the windows are double-glazed. The mezzanine bed and ladder were made from unmilled chestnut.

We worked with environmentally friendly materials whenever possible. Much of the timber was reclaimed or locally sourced and many of the fixtures and fittings recycled.

The book *Cradle to Cradle Design* by William McDonough was a huge influence. I did a lot of research into the materials used and their potentially negative effects on health and the environment and tried to find ways to avoid or minimize this. We used things such as "Auro Airfresh" paint and primer which claim to neutralize chemicals in the air that "off gas" from the building, a key subject in the book.

I'm now living in my wagon, feeling deeply satisfied, and I would like to network with people who identify with what we are doing and welcome any interest and inquiries.

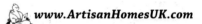 *www.ArtisanHomesUK.com*

The Shepherd's Hut

David Cherrington

BORN AND RAISED ON A SHEEP AND arable farm on the Wiltshire/Hampshire border, I first came into contact with a Shepherd's Hut at a very young age, as the farm used one as a field storeroom. (I used it more as an adventure den.)

> *"Born and raised on a ... farm on the Wiltshire/Hampshire border, I first came into contact with a Shepherd's Hut at a very young age ..."*

Years later I restored the hut for my children to play in, and once restored, people asked if I could source and restore huts for them. After looking into the second-hand market, I came to the conclusion that it would be more economical to build from scratch.

Using the original dimensions of 12-by-6 feet, we initially built a "Traditional Hut," with a stable door in one end and a single window at the side.

To increase our product range, we designed a hut with double doors on the side. Believing it would be ideal for fishermen on the riverbank, we named it the Fisherman's Hut.

To date we have built over 150 huts, for customers ranging from lords and ladies to a scrap metal dealer, from an Oscar-winning scriptwriter to an ex-supermodel, but I am especially pleased with the "Traditional Hut" we built for a shepherdess, a hut employed as originally intended.

> *"I am especially pleased with the 'Traditional Hut' we built for a shepherdess, a hut employed as originally intended."*

While enjoying working with my hands, I have never professed to be skilled and have benefited from the expertise of others, mainly Dean Widger, a self-taught craftsman with brilliant carpentry skills and an eagle eye for detail.

The Shepherd's Hut Company has always been client-led, so when we were asked for a hut that would accommodate a bed, mini kitchen, shower and toilet, we increased the size to 6-by-8 feet, sectioned off one end for the shower/toilet, and created a Tiny Home in the process.

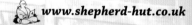 **www.shepherd-hut.co.uk**

> *"To date we have built over 150 huts, for customers ranging from lords and ladies to a scrap metal dealer ..."*

History of the Shepherd Hut

In the 19th century, farming customs on the light chalky soils of southern England were far different than modern day practices. Labor was cheap and plentiful, and there were no sprays or artificial fertilizers.

In order to get any kind of production from these thin and often-impoverished soils, fertilizer in the form of farmyard manure had to be applied. However, the physical problems and cost of hauling vast quantities of manure from the farmyard to the distant fields were too great.

To overcome these problems, farmers employed animals to do the work for them — sheep. The era of "The Golden Hoof" had arrived.

These sheep were not allowed to roam free, but were kept tightly enclosed behind hurdles. Once the forage crop or grassland had been grazed, the hurdles and flock would be moved on to new pasture, leaving behind manure that would be ploughed in for a crop of wheat, barley, or oats. Without this organic fertilizer, it would not have been possible to grow these crops in such light soils.

"...the shepherd was the most important worker on the farm."

If you owned a downland farm in the 19th century, a well-managed flock of sheep and a hard-working shepherd were essential; the shepherd was the most important worker on the farm. As most downland villages were set in valleys, and downland fields were the farthest away, the shepherd had to have somewhere to store his tools and medicines.

It was hard, physical work with flocks being moved daily, and the shepherd had to have somewhere to eat, rest and sleep, especially during the lambing season.

Thus, the Shepherd's Hut was born: a kitchen, dining room, bedroom, sitting room and storeroom all rolled into one. The old huts had a stove in one corner for warmth and cooking, and a window on each side so the shepherd could see the flock. A hinged stable door, which was always positioned away from the prevailing wind, enabled him to hear the flock, and strong axles with cast iron wheels were used to withstand the constant movement from field to field.

The durability of these huts is evident today, with many fine examples still being used by farmers, mainly as storerooms. They can often be seen parked alongside fields. Many more have been consigned to agricultural museums, giving testament to days gone by.

Roulotte in France

Jakob Seewald

I'M AUSTRIAN AND I MOVED to the centre of France one-and-a-half years ago, where it is sparsely populated and land is cheap. Currently, I live on my parents' organic farm with my dog Kiki until I can find the right place.

Until I was 25 years old, I had no idea what to do with my life. I had started studying economics, and then I traveled around the world.

> *"France has a more liberal view on living styles. Here I am able to live independently and freely…"*

One day, whilst working for a carpenter in Australia, I realized that working with wood was what I wanted to do.

So I returned to Austria, learned the trade, and later moved to the Creuse. France has a more liberal view on living styles. Here I am able to live independently and freely and this is where the roulotte comes in with its many benefits.

No building codes are applicable for a roulotte; plus it is movable, so wherever I go next, I can tow it with a tractor.

After a year and a half thinking about the design, it took me six months to build my roulotte. It measures 7.5 × 2.5 metres. The chassis is 1.2 m from the ground, and with the height of the roulotte built on top, it comes to almost 4 metres.

The chassis is around 50 years old and had been used for hay transport. I had to restore the wagon to support the weight, about 5 tons.

Natural and local non-industrial building materials are very important to me. I used locally milled wood; hemp insulation came from a nearby farmer, and the windows were made from an oak tree on our property.

Finishing touches like handles were reclaimed. The metal for the roof was cheap, but not flat. Running over it in my car solved that! I found the oven in a ruined house just waiting to provide my heating, cooking, and hot water.

> *"I used locally milled wood; hemp insulation came from a nearby farmer, and the windows were made from an oak tree on our property."*

> *"After a year and a half thinking about the design, it took me six months to build my roulotte."*

I designed the structure to meet my needs. I didn't want a high-level bed even though I have high ceilings. I took great care to build a beautiful ceiling—translated into English, it would be a basket bow with five middle points. I did all the woodwork, including the framing and cladding with Douglas fir. The doors, windows, and some of the interior work are oak.

For the last few weeks I have had running water, connected to a stone well with a small pump. What a luxury! After half a year of living in this wonderful shelter, I can say that winter is no problem with the oven going. I was lucky to find this wonderful place on top of a hill. There is nothing around me except an old ruin I am rebuilding with my father.

jaksee.webege.com

"*No building codes are applicable for a roulotte; plus it is movable, so wherever I go next, I can tow it with a tractor.*"

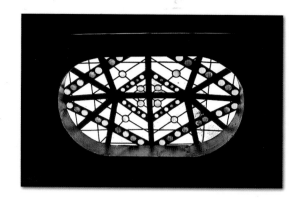

French Circus Caravan

Corinne Boyer

OUR SMALL FAMILY lives about 30 minutes north of Olympia, Washington. We have had this caravan since early August 2011. What a find! I have always wanted to live in or work out of a Gypsy wagon since I was a young teenager. My husband Claude and I were in the process of purchasing a piece of land when he found this caravan for sale. We worked on fixing it up for six weeks, certainly not a true restoration, but a definite improvement. Here is what we have learned about it:

It's from France and was brought to Guemes Island by retiring circus performers around 1992. They apparently paid 30K for it to come across the ocean. What I learned from the owners' neighbor was that the woman was covered in tattoos and the man was in the *Guinness Book of World Records* for something or another; they also drove a pink Cadillac. I found out the wagon is called a "showman's wagon," or in French *"Forain Roulotte."* It was used for show folk and traveling circuses. They are also called "Living Vans." This one was built in about 1945 and is one of the last of its kind. An excellent online resource can be found at ***www.travellerdave.co.uk***.

With the help of Dave, we think the caravan is probably from Belgium and was pulled by a World War II ex-military vehicle, although from different horse people, I have been told that it was definitely set up to be pulled by horses, probably a team of eight to ten.

It has all of the original fixtures, including skeleton keys that lock the cupboards and front door. It has a small cast iron sink in the kitchen area and plenty of built-in storage in each room. This wagon was built to move! The stove did not come with it, but is a French multi-fuel stove. We know that it must have had a coal stove originally. There are all of the old electrical outlets and switches, although the original fixtures are missing. It was built extremely well and has some unique handmade details, including the skylight that casts rainbows throughout the living area.

We have been temporarily living in this magical little space for the year, while getting ready to build. I teach weekly classes on herbal medicine and the wagon is a great classroom. When we move out into our new home, I will turn it into a full-blown herbal apothecary and continue my teaching.

Tiny Wooden Home on Wheels

Frank Belo

WHILE TRAVELING THE COUNTRY in an RV the last few years, building for cool folks along the way, my love of woodworking and the outdoors has only grown. Having a very healthy obsession with cabins and tree houses since my Lego and Lincoln Log days, I decided to sell my RV and build myself a mobile cabin (in Black Mountain, North Carolina).

My goal was to build a home using as many sustainable materials as possible. I started with a custom-built trailer that mimics a sub-floor in a stationary home— adding leveling jacks and threaded rod to anchor the walls down. Once I insulated the floor and screwed plywood down, it was just like building anything else—with special attention given to high winds.

The exterior is all cypress, coated with linseed oil and a hemp oil product with natural UV and mildew blockers. For insulation I used sheep's wool. While I got new lumber for the exterior and framing materials, I used reclaimed and free wood for the interior.

The flooring was made from scrap wormy maple sitting at the sawmill, with enough left over to rip down for the window trim. A scrap pile of cutoffs and unusable material from a portable sawmill clearing land nearby made for some great focal pieces once I planed them down.

The back wall is built of untreated pallets I collected around town. The kitchen has everything I need to cook and clean while on the road, and there is an instant hot water heater that has a showerhead attachment. The cabin has RV connections as well, so hooking up to a campground or friends' house is super convenient. I chose not to have a bathroom, since finding one on the road is not difficult; I figured that if I park somewhere long-term, a compost toilet in an outhouse would be fun to build.

It was a great experience building the home. My great friend Carch and his brother Jay each gave me a hand and my dog Dusty a paw, so a lot of love went into this. I hope others will enjoy seeing it.

I think it's important for people to have knowledge of natural building materials and finishes that will protect their homes while not destroying the lands around them. Hopefully this is the first of many microcastles I get to build. See you on the road!

Dimensions: 7′ × 10′ = 140 sq. ft.; height off road just under 10′

> *"My goal was to build a home using as many sustainable materials as possible."*

"I think it's important for people to have knowledge of natural building materials and finishes that will protect their homes while not destroying the lands around them."

"The back wall is built of untreated pallets I collected around town."

Little Yellow Door

Ella Jenkins

LIFE IN LITTLE YELLOW is wonderful. It's actually very much like normal, but without the things that used to bug me about living in other people's spaces. In fact, most everything that pissed me off or stressed me out in previous living situations is no longer problematic. I'm not stepping on anyone's toes, I can move or change whatever, whenever, and everything I love is organized all nice-like under one roof.

It's like the whole thing is one big relief. It's a relief to have a simpler life. It's a relief to have less things. It's a relief to be compact and contained. Like a hug, I like to think my house is quite like a hug.

I live on a little ranch down the hill from my landlords' house in a pretty wee field with a nice set of bushes and trees just beside; a perfectly adequate distance so as to be totally left on my own.

"I like to think my house is quite like a hug."

Storage and space in this house amaze me. I have many things inside, but I don't feel cramped and feel the need to fill it any further. Everything I've needed to find a spot for has one. It sounds a bit ridiculous to write it out, but all I can say is that it feels big to me.

It feels so big that I can barely think of Little Yellow as being as small as she is, and certainly not tiny. There were four people eating dinner in here the other night (myself included) and it felt no different than having three people for dinner anywhere else.

Maybe it's a magical house. Like that wacky carpetbag Mary Poppins had, where you could fill it far past its apparent capacity and still have room for your umbrella. Except that my house isn't made of carpet.

Working on this project through the build year, I got so bogged down in the process that I think I almost forgot that when it was done it would be my home. Every time I drive in and see the tiny little A-frame smiling at me with its tiny little porch light I get all proud and fuzzy.

I've found my house to be an unusual crossroads of exactly what I wanted and exactly what I needed. Perhaps I'm still in the honeymoon phase with Little Yellow, but I wouldn't live in anything else for the world.

"Maybe it's a magical house."

 LittleYellowDoor.wordpress.com

"It's like the whole thing is one big relief. It's a relief to have a simpler life. It's a relief to have less things. It's a relief to be compact and contained."

Kian's Mobile Home
Kian Clipson

"Perfectionism is a refusal to let yourself move ahead. It is a loop — an obsessive, debilitating closed system that causes you to get stuck in the details of what you are writing or painting or making and to lose sight of the whole.

Instead of creating freely and allowing errors to reveal themselves later as insights, we often get mired in getting the details right."

—Julia Cameron

I GUESS THE FIRST QUESTION I ASKED when building a house is "Where?" Where do I want to live? Where can I afford to live? And ultimately, where am I allowed to live? After thinking about it for a long time and realizing how restrictive these questions were, I chose to postpone answering them for a while. I decided to build my house on wheels so that it could come with me wherever I went.

I started by drawing out a few rough sketches but soon realized it was impossible to work out every little detail in advance and that I was going to have to just start, and work out the rest as I went along.

After eight months of working on the project every spare minute, it seemed to have taken over my whole life. I would stay up all night trying to figure out little weather-proofing details or how to make up the joinery. It's all I could think and talk about; it had become an obsession.

The barn where I was building the house was right on top of a big hill, up a narrow rocky track, with no electricity. I'd often get curious passers-by asking all sorts of questions. Some people just got it, they loved the idea of a house that could move — the freedom of a home you could take anywhere with you!

Then, there where those who were puzzled, and would ask, "But how will you get it down from here?" or "Do you need a

"I decided to build my house on wheels so that it could come with me wherever I went."

special license?" and the inevitable "Where's the toilet?" All these different responses made me realize that this house was not the most practical or sensible of ideas. In fact, to many it was just plain crazy. Yet it captured the imagination of certain friends and their enthusiasm was enough to motivate me though the seemingly endless finishing jobs.

Now I've finally moved in. It's been a long journey with lots of doubts along the way. I realize how when we get obsessive and bogged down in the detail, we can lose sight of the whole. Now when I look at the

house, the parts that I'm proud of and the places where I made mistakes are together an integral part of this happy home.

"Some people just got it, they loved the idea of a house that could move — the freedom of a home you could take anywhere with you!"

"Now I've finally moved in. It's been a long journey . . ."

"I was unhappy and trapped in a job I hated because I had a house I could not afford that I purchased right before the market crashed."

The Fortune Cookie
Kera, the Dreadnaught Darling

I HAPPILY BLAME MY FRIENDS, Adam and Suzi, for making me take an honest look at being more earth-friendly. It all started with cutting back on packaging, then a hard look at the foods I ate, next a deeper understanding of what businesses I was supporting…it goes on from there.

I think when you decide to take a more "green" approach to your life, there's a snowball effect. You see how everything is connected, from the planet, to the people, to the life you are choosing to live. I realized I had a choice to make. Going back to being a mindless consumer was rather unlikely, so I started making active choices that were better for me and the planet.

All of this came to a head. I had this 1,100 sq. ft. house and I had to live in the garage in order to make the mortgage payment. I rented out the rest of my rooms to try and cover expenses. I was unhappy and trapped in a job I hated because I had a house I could not afford that I purchased right before the market crashed. I felt really overwhelmed, and I just could not do it anymore.

I realized I wanted a small, portable home. For a few years I had been drooling over the Tumbleweed Homes, but later realized I wanted something a bit different. I found that Dee Williams had started Portland Alternative Dwellings (P.A.D.) and reached out to her directly.

She was very helpful and gave me a tour of her small house, but advised that P.A.D. was too busy to take an additional contract. I had mentioned in my first contact with her that I wanted something like a Tumbleweed Home with the styling of a gypsy *vardo*. She sent me to Abel Zimmerman, with the recommendation that he would do a splendid job and that he specialized in *vardos*. I was ecstatic.

I ended up quitting the hated job, selling the house, and using what money I had saved up to take a vacation and to contract Abel Zimmerman to build my beautiful home, The Fortune Cookie.

Riley, my Shih Tzu and I have been living in The Fortune Cookie for over a year now. I work for myself blogging, making synthetic dread falls and hair accessories out of The Fortune Cookie. I travel a lot and merchant on the Renaissance circuit. I am happier than I have ever been in my life. I make my own hours and live life at my pace. It is glorious.

You can follow my adventures at:
www.dreadnaughtdarling.com

Abel Zimmerman's *vardos*:
www.zylvardos.com

"I am happier than I have ever been in my life. I make my own hours and live life at my pace. It is glorious."

Mobile Workshop/ Overnight Camper

Tohner Jackson

MY TRAILER HAS BECOME THE symbol that makes me strive for simplicity. I wanted something that was a mobile workshop/ self-contained camper and I wanted it all in a relatively small space. One which I could perpetually try to perfect by filling the space with only tools that have multiple uses, so that most any woodworking project I would be likely to encounter, I could handle it between my trailer and truck. I wanted to stay away from specialty tools I would only need on limited projects. (I'm a homebuilder/custom woodworker.)

I also wanted to have a space that, if I was building a house in a remote location or traveling between projects, I would have a place to sleep, eat, and be sheltered.

Figuring that the bigger the space, the more of it I would fill, and the more of it I would fill, the more it would become cluttered, and the more it became cluttered, the more I would be in disharmony.

At the end of the day, my wish is to keep it simple: love, woodworking, family and in general a more simple life, and this trailer is my first step.

www.ArtisanBuilders.com
www.OneTreeWoodwork.com

"At the end of the day, my wish is to keep it simple..."

"I wanted something that was a mobile workshop/self-contained camper..."

"...most any woodworking project I would be likely to encounter, I could handle it between my trailer and truck."

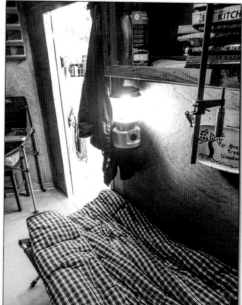

The Veggie Wagon
Eliot Coleman

Four Season Farm is an experimental market garden in Harborside, Maine, owned and operated by writers Barbara Damrosch and Eliot Coleman. The farm produces vegetables year-round and has become a nationally recognized model of small-scale sustainable agriculture.

THE "VEGGIE WAGON" WAS conceived as a way to set up more quickly at farmer's markets. It has been a great success. However, I have never created any blueprints. It was constructed from drawings and computations scribbled on odd pieces of paper, as first-time ideas usually are.

"We started with a 5′ by 8′ flatbed trailer. We used standard 2 × 4s to construct the frame of the building."

We started with a 5′ by 8′ flatbed trailer. We used standard 2 × 4s to construct the frame of the building. The boarding is tongue and groove for extra strength. We bolted the structure firmly to the trailer with metal strapping at all four corners. We added 2 × 4s in the metal slots at the front of the trailer for extra strength in case of

a sudden stop. To keep it light, the roof is not boarded, but rather just covered with a single layer of overlapping pine clapboards. The roof and trim are painted.

Originally the sides were varnished, but that didn't weather well and they have since been painted. The vegetable display shelves are hinged at the bottom and supported by lengths of chain when open. The sales table folds up against the back of the structure when it is all closed up.

"A wire brings power from the towing vehicle's cigarette lighter so we can plug in the cash register."

A removable mini-door covers the bottom of the door area at the rear and is used as a sales shelf, sitting on the trailer tongue at the front of the structure. The awning supports and fixtures are ¾-inch metal electrical conduit. The diagonal awning supports are removed and stored inside for transit. The awnings are rolled upon their bars and tied to those dangling cords. The veggie wagon now has a green-striped awning over the sales table in the back as well as over the veggies on the sides.

"To keep it light, the roof is not boarded, but rather just covered with a single layer of overlapping pine clapboards."

A wire brings power from the towing vehicle's cigarette lighter so we can plug in the cash register. We have recently added a "Four Season Farm" sign that runs along the peak of the roof. That is about it. If anyone makes improvements to this prototype, we would enjoy seeing a picture of what you create.

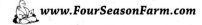 ***www.FourSeasonFarm.com***

The ArcStream

Addison Lanier

I WAS RAISED IN THE Albertan prairies where you'd think I would've had too much space. Who'd have thought I'd end up as a product designer finding ways to maximize it?

I guess I love the challenge of having lots of empty space even after I've put everything I could want inside it. Someone called me Mr. Extra-Spatial once, and it stuck. My designs either save space or cross-function: cell phones, folding bikes, a transit bus, corporate jet furniture, an auto ticket teller, ski racks, wine racks, double-duty tables, lamps, and mannequins. Then a few small condo designs inspired my line of SPACiOUS home conversion furnishings…"compact comfort with clever convenience" to save amazing amounts of space, time and money.

I renovated "ArcStream" (shown in these photos) inside with another invention of mine. ArcSys Frame is pretty much one device, a patented "construction curve" or metal "Arc," which people can snap-on to flexible sheet material. You can build many things with it, such as lightweight, humanely-shaped interior designs. ArcStream's meant to capture people's eye and imagination by showing what they can do with the Arc. It took me one year, and a small mountain of shiny objects that I'd found, to "cross-func" the inside of this 1970's Land Yacht. It's now a space-saving, sound-surrounded, steam-showered, star-observation, luxury-kitchen cave-on-wheels. ArcStream's maiden voyage was to Burning Man 2008, where the

year's theme was the American Dream. My helper Meghan put up a picket fence and served free apple pie out over the fake fold-up lawn. ArcStream lived in the center of Yaletown, Vancouver during the months when the city ramped up for the Olympics. ArcStream's been perched on a cliff overlooking a coastal cove, 40 minutes from my home by kayak, yet hours by car. Its Jetson-style luxury seems surreal when it's situated in rugged wild settings or in downtown "condo-forests."

We just can't get enough space, can we? A few years of fun inside ArcStream has helped me distill a design that I think sets a new precedent for "empty space vs. ultimate function." I'm keen to bring it to life with a client who has a roll/rail/float or fly project. Hey, bend the way you build!

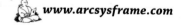 **www.arcsysframe.com**

"It's now a space-saving, sound-surrounded, steam-showered, star-observation, luxury-kitchen cave-on-wheels."

EL COSMICO

EL COSMICO IS THE latest lodging concept from Liz Lambert and her management company, Bunkhouse. El Cosmico, opened in the fall of 2009, extends Lambert's vision a few hundred miles west to an 18-acre plot of land in Marfa, Texas. "El Cosmico is part vintage trailer, safari tent, teepee hotel, and campground, part creative lab, greenhouse, and amphitheatre— a community space that fosters and agitates artistic and intellectual exchange."

Vagabond. Kozy Coach. Imperial Mansion. An armada afloat on a vast sea of desert. Our trailers from the heyday of nomadic recreation have been restored with marine-varnished birch interiors, furnishings collected from around the world, and amenities for a comfortable camp experience. Each trailer has a unique combination of cooking, dining, sleeping, bathing, and recreational features and comes equipped with fans and heaters, refrigeration, basic cooking supplies, and a radio with wireless iPod connectivity.

Each of our 22 ft. diameter tepees has brick floors and offers a queen bed, love seat, and small daybed, as well as lighting and an electrical outlet for charging devices.

Each wall tent is 120 sq. ft. and has wood floors, durable canvas walls and doors, and a zip-close screen option for airflow when desired. Safari tents come equipped with queen beds, a chair, simple lighting, and an electrical outlet for charging devices. In the winter, beds are heated with electric mattress warmers.

More than just a place to spend the night, El Cosmico offers opportunities for creativity and play. Our evolving program of workshops and retreats ranges from sewing to cooking to art classes to writing workshops and more. Over time, we will add a series of art shacks — a silkscreen workshop, a pottery studio, a darkroom, and others — places for both guests and locals to get their hands dirty. In addition to the Trans-Pecos Festival of Music and Love held annually onsite, our program of events and festivals is expanding to include film, music, and cultural events.

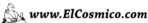

www.ElCosmico.com

Photos by Nick Simonite <*www.nicksimonite.com*>

"El Cosmico is part vintage trailer, safari tent, teepee hotel, and campground, part creative lab, greenhouse, and amphitheatre . . ."

Renovated Trailer in California Desert

Reanna Alder and Nathen Lester

MY HUSBAND AND I RENOVATED this 1962 travel trailer over a six-month period and moved in just before our wedding in May. The renovation was the most ambitious construction project either of us had undertaken, and involved removing and re-sealing all the exterior openings, repairing minor water damage, painting, rebuilding shelving, and installing a new floor. We also had to clear away a lot of rubbish at the north end of my husband's parents' property so that we had somewhere to park it. (That alone took three weeks.)

I have had a fascination with tiny homes for some time now. My husband graduated from school with substantial student loan debt, and we decided to move to Joshua Tree,

California, partly to live near my brother and sister-in-law and their new baby. We wanted to live in "toddling distance," as my sister-in-law put it, and also keep our monthly costs very low. Since the trailer was already parked on my in-laws' property (my husband lived in it for a while as a teenager!), our only costs were the renovation expenses as we went along.

The trailer living space is about 8′ wide and 24′ long. Our bathroom, fridge and chest freezer are outside, as well as a solar cooker and a stock tank for cooling off in the summer.

We have no plans to take the trailer on the road, but it's nice to know the possibility is there.

> *"The renovation ... involved removing and re-sealing all the exterior openings, repairing minor water damage, painting, rebuilding shelving and installing a new floor."*

My husband has a few blog posts that contextualize some of this, here:

www.shltr.net/thom-alder1
www.shltr.net/thom-alder2

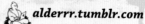 **alderrr.tumblr.com**

> *"The trailer living space is about 8′ wide and 24′ long."*

Yard cleanup

Stock tank "swimming pool"

Kitchen floor plan

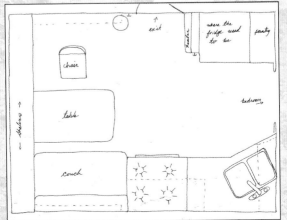

"We have no plans to take the trailer on the road, but it's nice to know the possibility is there."

Before and after

My Teardrop Trailer
The Blonde Coyote

Mary at 14,000 feet

I MAKE MY LIVING AS A FREELANCE writer and photographer and, since I can work from anywhere, I spend my winters house-sitting, and spring, summer, and fall on the road. I lived out of my car for 7 years in between house-sitting jobs until last year, when I bought a homemade Teardrop trailer for my 30th birthday.

"(It is)...5 feet by 10 feet, weighs about 600 pounds, and is a work of art."

My Teardrop, nicknamed "The Rattler" is 5 feet by 10 feet, weighs about 600 pounds, and is a work of art. I bought it from an 80-year old craftsman in Nebraska who made it in his garage using his own plans and design.

Inside, it has a full-sized bed, with storage space underneath, a fold-up table, eight square feet of floor space, drawers, cabinets, counter space, and a pop-up skylight. Outside, in the back, is a side out kitchen/galley area with plenty of

storage space for pots, pans, and food and a propane burner for cooking. I installed a 125-watt solar panel on the roof, which supplies all of the power for my mobile office.

The Teardrop may look tiny but it was actually a major space upgrade for me! Still, I'm ruthless about getting rid of anything and everything I don't need. When you live in less than 50 square feet, it's amazing to walk through a big box store and realize that whole sections of consumer culture no longer apply to your life.

People often ask me if I feel claustrophobic in such a small space—never! I have the whole world for a front porch! I think my favorite thing about living on the road in a Teardrop is that I'm always outside. I'm an avid hiker, climber and mountaineer, and being able to explore the world all day and sleep in my own bed every night is a vagabond's dream.

Since I bought the Rattler, it's seen a huge chunk of North America. So far we've rolled through 31 states, including my 50th state: Alaska! My Border Collie mixes, Bowie and D.O.G., both rescues, go everywhere with me. As far as they're concerned, the Teardrop is their rolling dog house.

This summer I'm perfecting the art of boondocking—camping for free on public land—in the great state of Colorado. When I'm not at the wheel or the keyboard, I'm outside exploring, climbing mountains, and taking photographs.

–Mary Caperton Morton
a.k.a. the Blonde Coyote

www.TheBlondeCoyote.com

Windmill Campsite, Oklahoma

"...it has a full-sized bed, with storage space underneath, a fold-up table, eight square feet of floor space, drawers, cabinets, counter space, and a pop-up skylight."

Garden of the Gods, New Mexico   *Mount Saint Helens, Oregon*

Salmon Glacier, Alaska   *Cedar Breaks, Utah*

Teardrop Kitchen   *Lost Coast, California*

San Antonio Dome, New Mexico

*"I have the whole
world for a front porch!"*

Sisters on the Fly

David Foxhoven

Jayne Kennedy

Howdy Lloyd and fine folks of Shelter Publications! I am a long-time admirer of your work, which has brought me so much joy and inspiration, and caused me to seek out and experience such fine and memorable environments as Pollywogg Holler!

I am very excited about your upcoming book, and wanted to turn you on to a few wonderful elements of the vintage trailering community, which has added so much to my life.

I am a member of an All-Girl gang called the Sisters on the Fly, which numbers over three thousand "Sisters" throughout the U.S.A., with a few Sisters in the UK, Canada, and Australia.

We are growing by leaps and bounds, and I am proud to be Sister #203. The group was founded by Maurrie Sussman and her sister Becky, who wanted to fly fish in remote areas with some level of comfort and security. They decided to share this idea with friends and family, inspired in part by their adventuresome mom, Mazie.

Over the years, it has blossomed into a terrific organization that empowers women of all ages, backgrounds, and life experiences to come out and camp together in a safe, generous, and joyful way. The key components of this "gang" are our trailers, which have been restored, modified, gussied-up, and decorated to the nth degree, often with fabulous murals to greet our fellow travelers with.

Our trailers are acts of creativity and love, and the hardest part of any of our adventures is packing out to head home. Many of the Sisters have made their vehicular villas so inviting that they prefer them to their regular homes, and it gives many of us a feeling of safety and calm to know that we have a place that will always shelter us within a community of inspired and empathetic gals.

The Sisters on the Fly are pleased to be able to utilize the talents, resources, and camaraderie of the group for charitable acts, in support of organizations like Casting for Recovery, which offers healing and therapeutic fly-fishing retreats for breast cancer patients and survivors.

We have hosted hundreds of events, large and small, all over the U.S., and we often caravan to events together, making "getting there" a good part of the fun as we add Sisters and their trailers to the rolling cavalcade. Bringing a mile-long caravan of these beautiful trailers into settings like Monument Valley or along Route 66 is a thing of awe and wonder!

The Sisters on the Fly has brought so much joy and adventure into my life, and I hope that readers of this book feel comfortable to talk with Sisters as you come across us in the wild—believe me, you will know us when you see us!

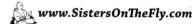 **www.SistersOnTheFly.com**

> *"Over the years, it has blossomed into a terrific organization that empowers women of all ages, backgrounds, and life experiences to come out and camp together in a safe, generous, and joyful way."*

David Foxhoven

David Foxhoven

"Many of the Sisters have made their vehicular villas so
inviting that they prefer them to their regular homes . . ."

David Foxhoven

Above two & right, Suzanne Cummings

More...

David Foxhoven

David Foxhoven

"I hope that readers of this book feel comfortable to talk with Sisters as you come across us in the wild—believe me, you will know us when you see us!"

All below, Suzanne Cummings

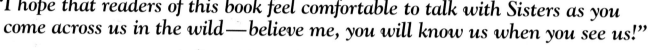

David Foxhoven

A Tomboy Gets Lots of Sisters

Sisters…I never had one that was blood. My sisters were the women that I admired as I grew into an adult: the teachers and coaches that touched my life, 4H leaders, and my grandmother.

One in particular was Pat. She was in high school when she took me under her wing; I was eight or nine. She taught me the finer points of showing cattle. She took me to shows, coached me, and listened to me as I struggled my way into being a teenager. When she went to college,

she was still my sounding board about boys and rebellion, school, and sports. She was a good listener and always gave solid advice. Way out in the boondocks, she was the closest thing I had to a real sister.

I grew up surrounded by men — my dad and my brother. I was as tomboy as you could get, but I was still a girl and they didn't seem to understand. Pat was a ranch girl, too, and I thought she was the most beautiful person I had

ever seen. She taught me about makeup and took me shopping for feminine clothes. I learned that girls can have horses, cows, and pickups, but they don't have to give up their feminine side. They can appreciate the outdoors, and when they find others who like the same things, they bond. This is a lesson I'm learning all over again from my Sisters on the Fly.

–Thea Marx (Sister #1323)

All below, Suzanne Cummings

The Cub—A Micro Shelter on Wheels

Designed, Built, and Decorated by Derek "Deek" Diedricksen

Deek Diedricksen is the guy who injects fun into the tiny house movement. He's a builder, designer, artist, musician, blogger — and he's prolific.

His book, shown above, is a charmer. It's a friendly, fun-filled, Mad-Magazine-inspired cartoon book of over 40 shacks, treehouses, forts, and whimsical designs — all of the tiny persuasion.

He was featured in Tiny Homes, and he got this home-on-wheels done just as were finishing up this book.

(Deek's website features a photo of him jumping in the air in front of one of his creations, and I asked him if he could do the same thing with The Cub. A couple of days later, the above came in an email.)

"My intention here was to come up with an EASY, affordable, and light travel trailer . . ."

114

"Total cost—around $2,000 or so (including a brand-new trailer, paint, hardware/decor). Total weight—1,520 lbs."

BUILT ON A STOCK, MAIL-ORDER trailer that's a mere 5′ by 8′, "The Cub" is a vacation house/camper on wheels that I built and designed in the summer of 2013. I've left it wide open—well, as wide-open as 40 square feet can be!—and without its intended downstairs mini-bed (that would double as a couch, and hidden storage), so that I could also use it as an attention-grabbing sales vehicle at flea markets, or for live music performances. Omitting a "downstairs" bunk also makes this camper visually larger, and keeps it less cluttered, which I prefer for the time being.

The side of this little rolling shelter also flips open so that the small, intimate space can connect with the larger outdoors when the weather allows, and a drop-down screen can be unfurled to keep the bugs at bay. The Tuftex-covered wall panel is lightweight and strong, and allows natural light into the structure while maintaining privacy, and at night, "The Cub" becomes a giant glowing lantern, illuminating the knick-knacks and colored glass bottles that reside on the shelves (also "the supports") of this moveable wall.

Using recycled materials is very important to me, and the back bead-board wall came from a nearby 100-year-old house. The ceiling is fabricated from re-purposed barn and fence wood—from a HUGE free score I came across. As for the art, yup, its free as well—the orange wall hanging is a 1970s stereo-cabinet door that I yanked off a trash pile and painted "blood orange," and the other green piece with a fossil in it was found on the side of the street on trash day in my town. Beyond that, about 25% of the framework 2 by 4′s were freebie castoffs from a construction site, and a few leftover from a HGTV shoot/build I hosted. A good deal of the paint and stain didn't cost me a penny either; I just scavenged it from a "Take it or leave it" shed at a recycling center.

My intention here was to come up with an EASY, affordable, and light travel trailer (one that can also incorporate a mini-bathroom on the trailer's tongue too!—accessed from the outside). "The Cub" plans are available on my website:

 www.relaxshacks.com

"The side of this little rolling shelter also flips open so that the small, intimate space can connect with the larger outdoors when the weather allows..."

"Built on a stock, mail-order trailer that's a mere 5′ by 8′, 'The Cub' is a vacation house/camper on wheels..."

Sumaya: A Little Piece of Sky

By Phil Duloy and Dan McMahon

Photos by Thomas Lay

I GREW UP IN WASHINGTON, D.C., raised by my English mother and Lebanese (step) dad. I named the trailer Sumaya (which is an Arabic name meaning little piece of sky), partly because it has a lot of windows in its sides and molly-crofted roof, and partly because it is made of cedar, which is the national symbol of Lebanon.

I had converted a 7.5m tonne Mercedes Benz to live in. That Benz served me well for seven years (and my mother-in-law happily stays in it today when she comes to visit), but I needed something a little bigger and nicer for my fiancée and newborn. I asked Dan McMahon, one of my best friends, to build the trailer for me as I haven't nearly the talents and skills required.

The ideas behind the trailer's construction came from discussions Dan and I had during the winter of 2008 while I was working as his apprentice on the construction of a large, green-timber-framed building in East Cornwall. We talked about what was important in a wheeled home a lot, as we both lived in our own similarly sized trucks at the time.

I was already living in Falmouth, Cornwall when Dan moved down and set up a

Dan McMahon and Phil Duloy

new workshop in 2009. By this time I had worked out what I wanted to do and had passed the assessment and training courses for a disaster relief agency called Shelterbox (*www.shelterbox.org*) and began deploying to disaster zones to distribute emergency shelter.

I spent seven of twelve months on deployments while Dan was working on various projects ranging from jewelry to artistic but extremely efficient wood-burning stoves.

October 2010 I asked him if he'd be willing to build me a trailer. He agreed, and we dug out the old plans and rehashed them. I bought a 30 ft. Ifor-Williams custom-built agricultural flatbed trailer rated to 3½ metric tonnes. Dan set to it with an angle grinder and welder, lengthening and strengthening it and adding compartments for its battery bank, water tanks, and under-floor storage.

Sumaya is hand-built, framed

in cedar, clad in the same, and the interior units are made of ash. The floor is oak. In the bedroom, Sumaya has a full-size double bed (which has gas struts to make access to the storage beneath it easier). There are two wardrobes, chests of drawers, and reading lamps.

Sliding, traditional Japanese-style doors separate the bedroom from the main cabin. There is a services cupboard below an additional, larger wardrobe. Across from this is the wetroom (which has a shower and a Swedish compost toilet). In the galley there is a catering-grade oven and sink. (My fiancée is a chef.) There is lots of storage space throughout.

Beyond the galley are the trailer's two exterior doors, and a seating area for up to 10 people around a large table. This can also be turned into a very large bed or play area.

The trailer also has:

- Solar charged battery bank (700 Ah)
- Concealed radiators with a central, easily adjusted thermostat
- SMD LED lighting with zoned dimmer switches
- KEF sound system with 8 ceiling-mounted drivers and two sub-woofers with an Alpine head unit
- Quality insulation for peace and quiet, as well as warmth
- Lots of (double-glazed) windows to admit natural light
- 13 amp sockets throughout (16 amp mains or from the roof-mounted solar panels)
- Running hot and cold water (200 liter fresh and grey tanks)

I can't help but feel extremely lucky to have this home built by my talented friend.

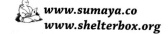
www.sumaya.co
www.shelterbox.org

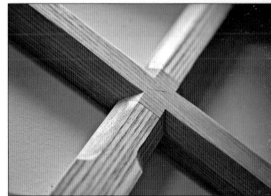

Phoenix Van
Robert Q. Riley

Sean Hellfritsch called our attention to this unique owner-built vehicle. The designer, Robert Q. Riley, is a mechanical engineer and industrial designer of low-energy-demand automobiles, as well as high performance watercraft, submersibles, hovercraft, and human-powered vehicles. His most recent work is the 225-mpg XR3 Hybrid.

Over 4,000 copies of the plans for Phoenix have been sold. Here is Robert's description of Phoenix:

ONE WOULD HARDLY GUESS THAT Phoenix was designed and built nearly 20 years ago, long before downsized vans were fashionable. Closed up for driving, Phoenix has the sleek look of a modern sports van. Its low frontal area coupled to a curb weight of only 2,000 pounds make it a low-rolling-resistance featherweight, even by today's standards. That, along with its VW van chassis, translates into 25-mpg highway fuel economy and nimble handling.

Nitrogen-cylinder-assisted gull-wing doors provide easy entrance into the low-profile cab. Two bucket seats in front allow central walk-through space into the rear. The rear is set up with bench seats along each side. Each bench seat has a lift-up top so food, clothes, and other bring-alongs can be stored underneath. Storage area totals about 14 cubic feet per side.

Phoenix expands tent-trailer style into a large room with stand-up height in the center for a six-foot adult. With the camper expanded, the section along each side that normally forms the back of the bench seat now extends out horizontally to become part of the bed (one bed along each side). Each bed measures 72 × 59 inches. Overall, the unit measures 12 feet wide across the bed area. The seat area is covered with three-inch-thick foam padding, which then serves as a built-in mattress when the camper is expanded.

Appliances are located across the extreme rear, above the engine cover. A sink is on the right, a mirror-faced ice box is in the center, and a two-burner propane stove is on the left. The stove uses disposable cylinders, which are the only kind legal in the absence of a power-vented stove hood. Water is carried in a 9-gallon plastic tank located under the ice box.

"Phoenix expands tent-trailer style into a large room with stand-up height in the center for a six-foot adult."

The cost to build Phoenix is about $2,000. For more information on how to build the body, go to: ***www.rqriley.com/frp-foam.htm***.

"The cost to build Phoenix is about $2,000."

Phoenix was first featured in *Popular Mechanics* magazine, in March, 1978. *Mechanix Illustrated* magazine featured a restyled version called "Renegade" in their March 1984 issue. Phoenix/Renegade was used as a background vehicle in the movie *Total Recall*.

Specifications

Length: 165″

Width: 72″

Width Expanded: 144″

Height: 71″

Track: 60½″

Wheelbase: 94½″

Body Construction: Fiberglass over foam composite

www.rqriley.com

"Its low frontal area coupled to a curb weight of only 2,000 pounds make it a low-rolling-resistance featherweight . . ."

Cricket Trailer

Garrett Finney

I saw one of these down by the beach recently. It's beautifully designed and executed. It does all sorts of delightful things. It's not cheap, but neither are Airstreams. Here is designer Garrett Finney's description of his invention:

CRICKET TRAILER IS THE COVERED wagon for the 21st century, an innovative and athletic travel trailer built to connect people to family, friends, nature, and adventure.

The Cricket story began with a boy's letter to Santa in 1972. This young boy, Garrett Finney, asked Santa for a houseboat. He didn't get one, but that letter began an enduring fascination with small environments. These intimate spaces, where the rituals of daily life feel more directly connected to the outside world, captured his imagination.

Fast-forward to 1999. Grown-up Garrett was a Yale-trained architect and designer. After stints living in Italy as recipient of the prestigious Rome Prize, England learning the blacksmith trade, and elsewhere in the U.S. as professor and designer, Garrett moved to Houston to work at NASA's Johnson Space Center—more specifically, working on designing the "habitation module" for the International Space Station (NASA-speak for the place where astronauts eat, sleep, bathe, relax—their home away from home).

But Garrett yearned to design things that would actually get built in his lifetime. He returned to Earth, not sure what would follow…

"…an innovative, lightweight, compact, and flexible small environment in which to travel and explore the world we live in."

Enter stage left: Cricket Trailer. The boy became a husband and father. He wanted to go on adventures and share his love of camping with his family. Combining his NASA experience with his love of the outdoors, Garrett worked to create an innovative, lightweight, compact, and flexible small environment in which to travel and explore the world we live in.

"Cricket is garage-friendly and towable by many 4-cylinder vehicles."

The result is Cricket.

Cricket is a high-quality tool—a travel trailer that is unique in terms of size, design, construction and functionality. It sits in the sweet spot between large, poorly constructed "McMansion" recreational vehicles and the humble, amenity-limited tent.

Cricket is garage-friendly and towable by many 4-cylinder vehicles. Its aluminum composite panel/laser-cut aluminum skeleton shell provides great insulation without warping, harboring mold, or off-gassing fumes (common problems for traditional trailers).

Cricket can be used off-grid with its solar-powered electrical system or connected to shore power. Its petite footprint packs many amenities: a lounge area that converts to bed; a bedside table that transitions to dining area; a kitchen with sink/counter/pantry; a porta potty and shower. Flexible opportunities are provided for stowing gear: 200 lbs. can be carried on the roof; the interior cabin provides locked storage and multiple attach points on ceiling and walls that can secure gear using simple bungee cords.

"Cricket Trailer is the covered wagon for the 21st century…"

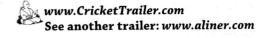 *www.CricketTrailer.com*
See another trailer: *www.aliner.com*

The Campa All-Terrain Trailer

This is an exceptionally tough and durable trailer for serious off-roaders. Here's what the company says about its units:

WE THINK THE CAMPA ATT is the best-engineered all-terrain trailer in the world, offering unmatched all-around capacity, versatility, durability, and performance. Our frame is manufactured from 3CR12 stainless steel (with 12% chromium) for high strength. The remainder of the Campa ATT is built from durable 304 L stainless steel. Our units are engineered and built to last a lifetime.

The toughest certifications to meet in the world are those of the Australian Design Rules [ADR] and the South Africa Bureau of Standards [SABS]. Campa is certified by both ADR and SABS. (South Africa and Australia are the two countries that pioneered the All-Terrain Camping Trailer concept decades ago.) Finite element analysis is conducted on all the trailer components, including the frame, and strict measures must be met to earn the coveted ADR certification.

The Campa ATT provides the best of both worlds with its off-highway and on-highway performance. One can crawl over the Rubicon Trail or travel at hustling highway speeds. A muscular frame and suspension design together with a fully articulating hitch provide overall stability. It is a functional, compact, and well-balanced system.

It can carry a ton, and has quick stopping power with the 12″ × 2″ electric brakes, as well as an integrated parking brake. The axle capacity is 6,000 lbs. and there is a 7,700 lb. capacity, fully articulating coupler.

The CUB is a new "entry-level" trailer, with less bells and whistles than the ATT, with a price of $9,500.

 www.campausa.com

The Whinny-Bray-Go
(Whinnies like a horse, brays like a mule, and goes down the road!)

"If it could break, it would, and it did!"

Lee Young — Captain Natural

From January, 1987 until November, 1988 I lived on the back of a horse heading for the wilds of Alaska, making my way on a trail from Arcadia, Florida. The ground was my bed nearly every night while on the trail—I was younger then! After an extended stay in Broken Arrow, Oklahoma, I was ready to continue my journey—my dream.

In Oklahoma, I made a trade with two old horse traders: my 1963 Mercury Comet for a wagon, mules, and harness—even-steven. After a wild learning period, I was broken in as a real muleskinner, and felt like I could drive a team anywhere.

Bits and pieces of this and that went into the construction of the original caravan—bein' a poor adventurer and all. The hubs were from a Rambler! It was light enough then to need only two little pony mules to pull it. The design was so I could live, work, and travel in a green mode of transportation.

I thought I had it together by the spring of '93 when I took the new wagon home on a 500-mile-round-trip shakedown run through Branson, Missouri, but I was wrong! If it could break, it would, and it did! The overall structure did well though.

I returned to Broken Arrow and rebuilt most of what I had already built. It took almost three months. A new paint job, new solid oak shafts, a rebuilt harness, and I added a little pup (trailer)—which was actually a sulky with the shafts shortened.

By early fall I was on my way to my next layover in New Mexico. It was great to have this camp already set up when crossin' the plains. The wind—Mariah—and the "Blue Northers" can be tough at times.

There the mountains put a stop to my progress; this turned out to be yet another major overhaul period—actually several over the next year or so. A new set of shafts made from electrical E.M.T. helped the mules by lightening their neck

"The Whinny served its purpose well for about four years and we traveled about 3,000 miles of hard trail together!"

weight by 40 lbs. I added a cab to ward off the snow and rain. While traveling this way, you learn many things. Foremost: always do somethin' to move ya forward whenever ya have the time. So, changes were made on a constant basis. The only true constant in the universe is CHANGE!

In the fall of 1995, the Whinny-Bray-Go was still on all fours — most of the time — when we clippity-clopped into Arizona. A fourth mule was added because I'd also added a new pup and a goat. The pup carried a 55-gallon plastic water barrel, which weighed 450 lbs.

Movin' this menagerie through Nevada to Utah was a job. At the height I managed five mules, two horses, two dogs, and a goat. Had it down to a science for the most part and was pretty darn efficient, and somewhat comfortable.

In the Bryce Canyon area of Utah, I stripped the Whinny down to make room for customers: adventure tours of a large ranch complete with a buffalo herd and ancient Native American ruins. That was just for the summer though.

The final resting place for the Whinny-Bray-Go was Panguitch, Utah, where I sold the wagon to a museum owner. After the Whinny was retired, it was back to horseback and living on the ground — well, I did have a cot to sleep on. The Whinny served its purpose well for about four years, and we traveled about 3,000 miles of hard trail together!

"While traveling this way, you learn many things. Foremost: always do somethin' to move ya forward whenever ya have the time."

Bear
the Tinker

In April 2013, I saw a post on the Tiny House Listings website with a gypsy caravan for sale for $6,000:

"A five-year-old, traditionally built utilitarian gypsy caravan, 6 × 12 feet and built on an original 1905 McLaughlin undercarriage — significant, because this was designed to carry glass milk bottles on rough roads. The ride on this wagon is smooth and comfortable when compared to other gypsy wagons.

This wagon has ample storage — located under the double bed platform, under the double bench seats, and also along the wall is a shelved cupboard....

There is a hideaway table with a painted-on checker/chess board. The one small contemporary convenience is a small unobtrusive solar light.

A gypsy wagon is not built to be pulled behind a vehicle, but rather to go at horse speed. The front can be removed so that a team or yoke can be hooked up. Thus you can pull it short distances with a contemporary vehicle.

To move the wagon long distances, it can be transported on a flatbed or behind a 1,500-pound (or larger) horse.

The covering tarp is military grade and is removable when it comes time for ordinary upkeep.

The wagon has a wood stove. It is not insulated; rather it is built in the old way with pretty interior panels and a covering tarp.

> *"Building the caravan was a dream that came about after my children grew up and left home."*

When the winter comes to those who choose the traditional lifestyle, a field is located, 200 bales of hay are ordered and, when delivered, are stuffed under and piled around the wagon. Only the front and rear end are left open for light. The hay is fed one bale at a time to the horse and by spring, when the insulation and the feed are gone, the wagon is pulled away."

> ## "For about 8 years I was a true nomad living by my wits on the roads of New Brunswick and Nova Scotia."

Note: *I've had a sort of whirlwind few days talking and corresponding with Bear, as well as his good friend and webmeister John Irving, and looking at videos and photos of him and his life. It was getting to know someone real well in a short space of time. Bear's outlook on life and his skills are unique in this day and age, and he obviously spreads good will everywhere he goes. I asked him if he could write something about his life, and he replied:*

"I was on the road as a farrier shoeing horses for 20 years. Building the caravan was a dream that came about after my children grew up and left home. For about 8 years I was a true nomad living by my wits on the roads of New Brunswick and Nova Scotia.

I performed as musician and story-teller at fairs and markets, cultural gatherings, and festivals. I also made and sold jewelry and handmade bows and arrows and taught traditional skills, yurt building, traditional archery, and plant and herbal lore. I also did talks on matters of the spirit world.

I could fill volumes, a lifetime's memories of horses and hounds, hunting and fishing, of good friends and many campfires and stories that drifted through the night and began again… Traveling in the spring and summer, and paths I've crossed.

Then in early fall finding a place for the long winter camp where I'd hide and hunt — to emerge again in spring when I'd get on the road again. And on my new rounds…there would be fields for my horse and caravan."

"I could fill volumes, a lifetime's memories of horses and hounds, hunting and fishing, of good friends and many campfires and stories that drifted through the night…"

More…

> "Being out on the road with the caravan, all the elements that I love are there: the outdoors, my horse, freedom, and I don't have to pay taxes. No mortgage, no rent."

A short video of Bear and his caravan was made by CBC, an episode in Wayne Rostat's series, On the Road Again. *Here's what Bear said in the interview:*

"In 1972, I looked at an article in *National Geographic* on gypsies. I turned to this page and there was this gypsy caravan, and it was like a flash — that's what I want to do.

Growing up as a kid, I was sort of an outcast and spent more time in the woods than I spent around people. When people finally saw me emerging from the woods, they said, 'The bear has come out of the woods,' and the name stuck.

I grew up on a farm. Being out on the road with the caravan, all the elements that I love are there: the outdoors, my horse, freedom, and I don't have to pay taxes. No mortgage, no rent. What's in it is mine.

It's a traditional life. A tinker by definition is a traveling tinsmith who mends pots and pans, and sharpens knives and axes; any sharpening job. I'm also a blacksmith/farrier; I shoe horses.

I'm about in the 1740s to the 1760s; I live in that time. I don't step out of character. I wear traditional clothes year-round.

When I'm out on the road I have to watch for cars and buses and look past the modern things and sometimes shut them out, but in my head I just try to avoid being disturbed from my time period.

I think my world is a better place. I'm escaping a world I don't agree with. I don't have to participate in it; I refuse to participate in it. The idea that everything is expendable just for the sake of profit, and to throw out traditional culture just for the sake of progress, doesn't make sense.

I've always been fascinated by history, I was raised by my grandparents. They were always storytellers; in the kitchen, when I was a boy, I had a little rocking chair right beside my grandfather's, and we'd sit by the wood stove, and storytelling was the way to pass the time.

Some people think I'm poor. One lady, she says to me, 'You're poor.' I said, 'What makes you think I'm poor?' She says, ' Well, you don't have a TV.' *(Laughter.)*

People who think I'm poor make a mistake. It's the people who have no dreams that are poor."

**YouTube video:
www.shltr.net/thom-bear**

www.BearTheTinker.com

> "People who think I'm poor make a mistake. It's the people who have no dreams that are poor."

The wagon was sold because Bear had a triple bypass and needed to settle down. These days he's living in the woods near Gananoque, Ontario, Canada next to 6,000 acres of protected forest land. He is available to perform music or storytelling at festivals, community, and cultural events, and also conducts workshops on traditional archery and yurt building. He makes traditional archery bows by hand, using locally sourced materials; they are available for purchase.

> "I'm escaping a world I don't agree with. I don't have to participate in it."

"I'm about in the 1740s to the 1760s; I live in that time. I don't step out of character. I wear traditional clothes year-round."

About a year ago, I was riding my Stumpjumper bike down a long local winding road when I heard "On your left," and a young wild longhaired guy on a bike came flying past me. I mean flying — fast. No helmet.

After he flew past, my jaw dropped even further as he started jumping. Front wheel up, back wheel off ground, rotate in air, lining up so landings properly oriented. Breathtaking, this level of skill and athletic grace.

I caught up with him at the bottom: Trevor "Ratman" Perlson, age 18. Turned out he and his buddies are outdoor adventurers, and Trevor introduced us to Ryan, who wrote the following about his camping trips on his unique motorcycle-with-mountain-bike rig.

—LK

Two-Wheeling It
Ryan Worcester

THE MINIMALISTIC exercise in nomadic living pictured here was born out of the fundamental desire to make the most of what I had and what I wanted to do — a love for two wheels and the magnetically charged push that is the deeply ingrained human desire to explore — and essentially was created as way to see a vast and diverse country with limited means. The bike was fitted with a very budget-minded, DIY-style pannier luggage system, and matching DIY custom-designed bicycle rack.

I've had some blissful, stunning, perfect days with this rig. I've also had some challenging, exposed days weathering conditions that ranged from desert heat to gale force winds, pelting rain, ice, and snow. After spending much of my life in the snow and isolated mountain regions in frigid, numbing, frostbite-inducing temperatures, still the coldest I've ever been in my life has somehow been on this motorcycle.

The minimal capacity to carry possessions forces you to jettison superfluous items and, as a result, be more exposed, connected, and immersed in the experience.

My principal cargo didn't even consist of a tent, but rather Spartan protection of a bivy sack with a sleeping bag (damn right, it's a compromise!). Small cook stove and pot, a few changes of clothes, camera, couple of books, repurposed ski clothing for the cold weather, a small toolkit, and a dry pair of clothes. And the bicycle, of course.

Placing ideals over comfort always has its perils, but the rewards are just about always worth it.

"The minimal capacity to carry possessions forces you to jettison superfluous items..."

"Placing ideals over comfort always has its perils, but the rewards are just about always worth it."

"The Wave," Coyote Buttes, AZ

Mt. Shuksan, WA

Motorcycle/Camping Trip from Canada to South America and Back

Bruce Baillie

23,000 Miles on a 1969 Moto Guzzi

I met Bruce while I was on Vancouver Island shooting pictures for Builders of the Pacific Coast. *(There's a picture of him and his mom on page 89.) I knew he'd since taken off on a trip to South America on an old Moto Guzzi, but didn't realize the extent of his travels until he pulled up in my driveway a few months ago in leathers on his 44-year-old Italian motorcycle. We downloaded over 1,000 photos from his camera, we had some lunch, and he took off for points north.*

Bruce is a guy of big actions and few words, and here's his condensed version of a very gutsy and very adventurous trip.

—LK

Bruce in 1994. Friends called him ZZ Bruce.

Bruce outside Shelter Publications' World Headquarters, February 2013

MY OLD MOTO GUZZI MOTORCYCLE is from 1969. Found on the Internet for sale in Florida, it has a later model 850 cc engine and four-speed transmission and drum brakes. A distributor and points ignition, very simple engineering. Hard to break, easy to diagnose and fix.

I had it shipped to Washington State and picked it up there. Added new tires, a new starter motor, rebuilt the carbs and added new aluminum saddlebags. Rode it around for a week with no problems, so left for Mexico.

"Headed down Baja to La Paz, took a boat to Mazatlan— all of west coast of Guatemala, El Salvador…"

Coil died in Oregon so replaced it with one from a '62 Ford in San Francisco. Headed down Baja to La Paz, took a boat to Mazatlan—all of west coast of Guatemala, El Salvador, was then held up by border guards when entering Honduras—they extracted a large bribe so that I could get my papers back.

Ferry from La Paz, Baja California to Mazatlan, mainland Mexico

"My old Moto Guzzi motorcycle is from 1969. Found on the Internet for sale in Florida…"

On to Nicaragua, Costa Rica, Panama. A hostel in bustling Panama City offered a boat to Columbia, four days later in Porto Belo, left for a four-day trip from eastern Panama to Cartagena, Colombia. Fantastic scenery, roads, and cities. Then to Ecuador, where the transmission gave out. One month there for new transmission, then on to Peru.

Coast road to Lima and then to Nazra, eastward to Cusco and Machu Picchu (great road). Got robbed, lost papers, and passport. On to Lago, Titicaca, and Bolivia, back to La Paz, met up with a Dutch friend with similar Guzzi and rode to Potosi and Sucre for a few weeks.

On to Uyuni and salt flats, then westward through the mountains in to Chile (bad roads—sand, gravel, ruts, washboards, and dust like talcum powder), 4,000 meters high and cold as hell. Down into expensive Chile, then east again through the Andes to Argentina, then south to Buenos Aires.

Run off the road many times and tried to sell the bike—no go. So up through Uruguay for a week, then to Brazil. Second day, there was a big bike meet on the coast, and as the only foreigner, I was very popular.

Headed north on beautiful coast road to Rio de Janeiro, beautiful city, good times. Enjoyed the entire coast of Brazil to Venezuela where gas is a penny a liter, but bank card not working, so back to Cartagena, Columbia to team up with two Argentineans and an American on bikes. No boats available so on to Turbo where a speedboat took us on a five-hour ride into Panama.

There was a nine-day wait in an isolated and heavily guarded town before a decrepit and overloaded cargo boat took us and the bikes in a six-day run up the coast to a place that had a road, and back we go to Panama City. Ran into major paperwork hassles in Costa Rica and Nicaragua, which forced me to ship the bike to Miami and ride from there across the U.S.A. to San Francisco, then north to Canada. 23,000 miles, five rear tires, two front tires.

Unloading Guzzi from boat, Cartagena, Colombia

La Paz, Baja California

Curious onlookers always

Machu Picchu

Machu Picchu

Coast of Peru

Near Medellin, Columbia

Uyuni Salt Flats, Bolivia

High in Andes, Bolivia

High mountains, Chile

Baños, Ecuador

Lush greenery north of Rio

Ferry (typical) on Amazon, Brazil

Anteater, huge claws, Brazil

Welding shocks, northern Columbia

Bruce traveled with Dutch cyclist Paul van Hoof in Colombia. Here Paul naps while Bruce repairs his throttle cable.

Yungas Road, the "Death Road" in Bolivia. "They say over 1,000 people die on this road each year, but I found it rather boring. Of course if you go over the edge, it's all over."

"Headed north on beautiful coast road to Rio de Janeiro, beautiful city, good times."

Taken from Sugarloaf Mountain in Rio de Janeiro." What a beautiful city!"

Seaside town south of Rio on coast. "The coast south of Rio is beautiful beyond description."

The Tricycle House

People's Architecture Office

THE TRICYCLE HOUSE addresses the theme "The People's Future" for the 2012 "Get It Louder" Exhibition in Beijing.

Private ownership of land in China does not exist, and The Tricycle House suggests a future temporary relationship between people and the land they occupy. In a crowded Chinese city, single-family homes can be affordable and sustainable, parking lots are used at night, and traffic jams are the norm.

"Private ownership of land in China does not exist..."

As a construction method, we experimented with folded plastic. Each piece of the house is cut with a CNC router, scored, folded, and welded into shape. The plastic, polypropylene, can be folded without losing its strength. Therefore, the house can open up to the outside, expand like an accordion for more space, and connect to other houses. The plastic is translucent, allowing the interior to be lit by the sun during the day or street lamps at night.

The Tricycle House is human-powered and operates off the grid. Facilities in the house include a sink and stove, a bathtub, a water tank, and furniture that can transform from a bed to a dining table and bench to a bench and counter top. The sink, stove, and bathtub can collapse into the front wall of the house.

www.peoples-products.com
www.peoples-architecture.com

Of related interest —
a variety of bike trailers:
www.wicycle.com

"The plastic, polypropylene, can be folded without losing its strength."

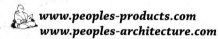

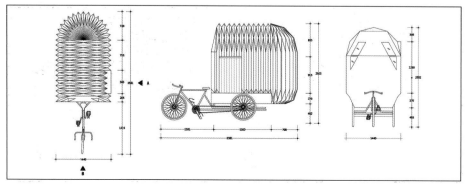

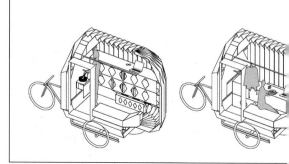

"The Tricycle House is human-powered and operates off the grid."

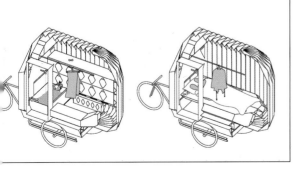

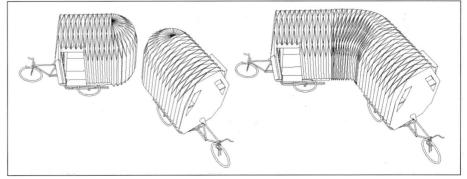

Why Buy When You Can Make!

Mark Hansen

"Small helps me focus on what is truly important and makes living with less more enjoyable."

I met Mark in spring, 2012 when I went back to speak about tiny homes at The North House Folk School on the northwestern shores of Lake Superior in Minnesota. Mark was the early founder of the school, a teacher of building birch bark canoes, and an accomplished designer and builder. He's one of those rare guys that can work in all materials.

His shop is a builder's dream. You feel it as soon as you enter: a fire burning, small birch bark canoe models in the rafters, wood tools, drafting tables, industrial sewing machine, work benches....

As I hung out with Mark, I kept discovering different items that he had built, and asked him to write them up — as he's done in the pages that follow.

–LK

This 14-foot birch bark canoe was the last of a number of such I made in the '70s, '80s, and '90s.

This sailing kayak trimaran uses bat-wing sails like Frederick Fenger's Yakaboos, which are oceangoing canoes and multipurpose sailing vessels of the Pacific Ocean.

These basswood carvings watch over my shop. Thank you, Harley Refsal, for getting me started with Norwegian flat plain carving!

The Beluga is a cargo kayak of stitch and glue plywood construction, 22′ in length and 30″ of beam. It is stable and capable of large open-water crossings.

This railroad bike was great fun for us in the 1970s. Wendy and I lived on a remote 40-acre homestead in Jonsdale, Minnesota from 1976-1980. It was 10 miles to town by road and 5 miles by railroad tracks. The tracks worked out just fine, even if we were trespassing!

We built this 22′ Mackinaw boat from Nelson Zimmer's lines at The North House Folk School over a six-month period.

Mark and Wendy

THE JOY OF DESIGNING and building captured me early on. Tree houses, forts, rafts, small boats, railroad bikes, etc. These were great learning opportunities on many levels. My primary interest has always focused on making useful things for meeting everyday needs.

In the past 20 years, small shelters under 100 sq. ft. have been of particular interest to me. They help me find the muse and don't require volumes of time and resources. Plus, small is relevant to our future. Add to this the idea of portability, and the creative options are multiplied.

Small helps me focus on what is truly important and makes living with less more enjoyable.

So here are a few ideas for now — I keep meaning to document these and other projects in more detail, but for now I am focused on building. I hope there's enough here to give you some ideas — see what you come up with.

Enjoy!
Mark

P.S.: Thanks, Shelter, for the valuable work you have offered all these years.

Dan

The Dan Van

THE DAN VAN IS A getaway land yacht that provides living arrangements for my son Daniel Hansen, a writer, poet, and graphic artist, who happens to have a neuromuscular disease. The design features are unique and specific to Dan's needs and abilities.

A Mercedes-Benz cargo van was the best choice for customizing a four-season live-aboard coach. The miles-per-gallon is decent and improves with lower speeds; there's a great engine and a drive train large enough to operate an electric wheelchair fore and aft.

We purchased a stripped-down 2500 van, a ¾-ton, five-cylinder diesel, 24 feet long, with 6′4″ of beam and 6′5″ of headroom.

The accommodations are for two. Important features include an overhead hoist, shower, composting toilet, 110-volt and 12-volt refrigerator, alcohol and electric stove, 110-volt hot water heater, solar hot water heater, LED lighting, and a wood-burning stove for cooking and heating.

There's a 100-watt solar panel, two 40 amp-hour AGM (glass mat) batteries, a charge controller, inverter, charger, 110 air conditioner, and a computer desk.

There is a full-length aluminum roof rack that includes a tent platform, a rack for storage, solar panel mounts, and awnings.

As in all small, thoughtfully designed spaces, the more time you spend in it, the better it serves you.

" . . . there's a great engine and a drive train large enough to operate an electric wheelchair fore and aft."

More...

Nipigon Tent

I DESIGNED AND SEWED THIS TENT FOR THE PURPOSE of living on Lake Nipigon (northwestern Ontario, Canada) in the winter while conducting caribou surveys for the Ontario Ministry of Natural Resources.

I've traveled this sub-arctic lake for 27 years and have made and used various tents, yurts, and lodges, but this 49 sq. ft. dome tent is my favorite. It is double-walled construction with Egyptian cotton interior wall and a silicone-impregnated nylon exterior wall; it's very warm and lightweight at 14 pounds.

The frame is aluminum tubing, and the half-moon doors can be zippered in multiple ways to regulate temperature inside. Temperatures in this area can get down to 50–60° below zero. In order to live comfortably at these temperatures, I use a titanium wood stove made by Four Dog Stoves. One armload of standing dead black spruce per day provides cooking, heat, and bathing water on a daily basis; the stove weighs eight pounds.

The more comfortable your living quarters are, the less food you need to stay warm on early mornings and evenings. There's also a solar benefit during sunny days.

When I blow out the candle at 8 P.M., the down sleeping bag is my shelter and the evening's warm bath and good supper in my belly is the furnace that keeps me warm through the night — cozy, warm, and relaxed.

Although the Nipigon tent was designed for lightweight travel for myself and gear with comfort, I have had company — but it's a bit too tight. It has 6′3″ standing headroom that serves as a drying loft for wet clothing and gear. The 7′ × 7′ footprint allows room for a 30″-wide bed, folding chair, and gearbox.

I've pulled this outfit on various carriers: toboggans and various sized *komotiks* (Inuit sleds) powered by myself, dogs, or a snowmobile — depending on the routes to cover and lake conditions.

This tent has served me well for 12 years, with the usual repairs and upgrades. A word of caution is always in order when using wood stoves in tents; a book could be written on this subject alone.

> *"The more comfortable your living quarters are, the less food you need to stay warm on early mornings and evenings."*

These homemade birch skis are an old Sami design, with handcrafted bindings for Mukluks.
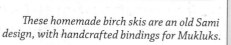

"The 7′×7′ footprint allows room for a 30″-wide bed, folding chair, and gearbox."

Here I am traveling on Lake Nipigon with 10 Greenland dogs using my Greenland komotik.

"It is double-walled construction with an Egyptian cotton interior wall and a silicone-impregnated nylon exterior wall…"

More...

Norwegian Pilot Cruiser "Aakvik"

I TOOK THE LINES FOR THIS sailboat from a pilot boat on the northwest coast of Norway and modified them for freshwater sailing on Lake Superior.

This live-aboard "pocket cruiser" is home for my wife, Wendy, and me for living on the lake during the summer months. It is 22 feet length overall, has 7 feet of beam, with 30″ draft.

I rigged Aakvik with a Chinese junk sail for its simplicity, ease of handling, and durability. There is approximately 45 sq. ft. of floor space, including the cabin and cockpit. I spent days mocking up various arrangements for two in a sitting headroom cabin, and after 10 years of sailing her with modifications, the cockpit and cabin are a pleasure to live in.

The accommodations for two include: 12 gallons of fresh filtered water, a gimbaled propane stove, composting head, berth for two, couch, seat, counters, and a navigation table.

The cockpit can be completely covered from the hatch to taffrail, which provides the necessary stand-up headroom and allows being snug when the weather "picks up." Like any small living space, Aakvik provides comfortable seats and berths for reading, writing, standing, and necessary space to move around in while underway.

There are two surfaces for meal preparation and another for other uses, and organized storage that is accessible and large enough for approximately 500 items necessary for sailing and living aboard. Wendy has often commented that "…the longer I live on Aakvik, the larger it seems."

Other features are:

- cold-molded construction fiberglass (breaking skim ice in the spring)
- 5 hp Honda long-shaft outboard motor well
- *yolow* (Chinese sweep) for human propulsion

Aakvik has taught me a great deal about Lake Superior, sailing, living in small spaces, and how much I love having Wendy on board.

"I rigged Aakvik with a Chinese junk sail for its simplicity, ease of handling, and durability."

"It is 22 feet length overall, has 7 feet of beam, with 30″ draft."

"Like any small living space, Aakvik provides comfortable seats and berths for reading, writing, standing, and necessary space to move around in while underway."

More...

Gypsy Wagon

THIS NOMADIC HOME has a long history of wandering, ranging from the ancient gypsy societies of Europe to the sheepherders of the American West.

The intent of the wagon is to be a getaway for extended periods of time with a high level of comfort for my wife, Wendy and me. We love to spend time on the shores of Lake Superior at all times of the year.

> "...a getaway for extended periods of time with a high level of comfort..."

This 6′×12′, 72 sq. ft. home rides on a 5th wheel carriage for smooth highway travel. (The carriage and a compact wood stove were built to specification by my friend, Donn Eliasen.) The interior is surprisingly roomy due to the 7° angle of the walls and curved ceiling. Increased under-storage is provided by the wagon's unique height and shape.

Wrap-around windows on all four walls help bring the outside into the living space. The gypsy wagon includes what I consider the following essentials for livable small spaces:

- comfortable bed for two
- windows with 360° view
- comfortable seating for two
- walls canted out to 7° angle at top
- two working surfaces
- insulation for coolness and warmth
- bug proof!

On the right is a solar-powered sauna, which folds up under the chassis when not in use. Made of ⅜″ double-wall polycarbonate greenhouse glazing, Mark said that on a day when the temperature was 5 degrees below zero, it was 120 degrees inside. The shadow you see inside is an 8-gallon aluminum kettle that provides hot water.

> "Wrap-around windows on all four walls help bring the outside into the living space."

> "The interior is surprisingly roomy..."

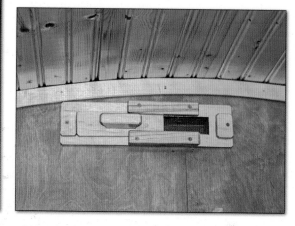

Micro Wagon

THIS LITTLE FELLA IS A REAL KICK! The micro-wagon — with a range of options — was fun to design and build. It may even make you willing to change your mind about how much space you really need or want for traveling.

The wagon was designed to ride on a 125-pound Yakima Rack and Roll trailer. This is a superbly built aluminum rolling platform capable of hauling 400 pounds.

The interior living space is 4′ × 7′ with a total of 28 sq. ft. The bolted-on hut is detachable from the wagon, and at 250 pounds, can be easily placed wherever space is livable off the trailer. The intended use of this light wagon is for my wife and me to make quick getaways around Lake Superior, utilizing a small footprint.

The Micro Wagon has comfortable sleeping and sitting for two people and includes two separate work surfaces for food prep, etc. The total weight of the rig is 375 pounds, which can easily be pulled by an economy car.

"The wagon was designed to ride on a 125-pound Yakima Rack and Roll trailer."

I have prepared plans that include the following:

- detailed drawings and three perspectives
- step-by-step instructions with photographs and drawings
- materials list, sources, cost estimates
- mold construction details
- tool list
- window, door, latch construction
- ideas for use
- list of necessary items to live comfortably abroad
- alternate designs and construction methods

www.ThinkSmallDesigns.com

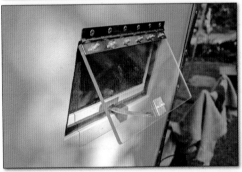

"...for...quick getaways around Lake Superior, utilising a small footprint."

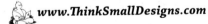

WATER

Tara Tari
Capucine Trochet

In January 2013, we got an email from Justin Anthony, telling us about a 30-year-old French woman, Capucine Trochet, sailing the high seas in a little sailboat single-handedly — with no engine and no GPS.

It took months to track her down, and for the last four months we've had off-and-on emails — whenever she was in port somewhere. It's been a huge adventure for her — a book could be written about these risky and remarkable journeys, and about this brave and remarkable person.

In 2010, French engineer Corentin de Chatelperron built a boat in Bangladesh based on local fishing boats, using jute (instead of fiberglass), polyester resin, and recycled materials. It was about 27´ long by 6´ wide. He christened it Tara Tari and sailed it 4,500 miles from Bangladesh to Marseille. He exhibited the boat in shows in France and was eventually contacted by Capucine Trochet. They were kindred spirits, and the next year, Capucine began her adventures on Tara Tari.

In November, 2011, Capucine left Marseille (southern France) in Tara Tari for Barcelona, then sailed along the Spanish coast in strong winds, then through the Strait of Gibraltar,

All photos © Capucine Trochet

where the Mediterranean meets the Atlantic.

She sailed with no engine, using paper charts, a compass, and the barest of equipment. Everywhere she stopped, people were intrigued, and helped her: food, shelter, repairs.

Capucine arrived in Lanzarote in the Canary Islands in May 2012, exhausted, and returned to France to recuperate and see her family.

She came back to the Canaries in November,

2012, when the trade winds were blowing, to continue her journey across the Atlantic. This time her friend Maxime sailed with her, and together they sailed to the Cape Verde Islands (roughly off the coast of Senegal), then across the Atlantic some 2,500 miles to Martinique (near Puerto Rico).

On the following pages are photos and stories from Capucine about her adventures.

> "She sailed with no engine, using paper charts, a compass, and the barest of equipment."

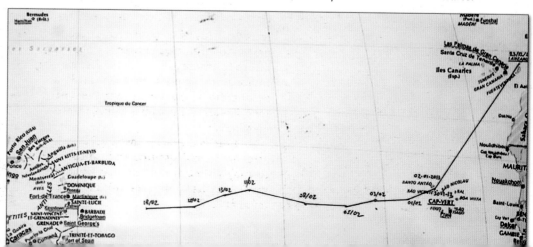

THE OCEANS REPRESENT OUR future, and as such we should care for them as we would a treasure or person that we love.

For the last 7 months, I have been living a great adventure on board *Tara Tari,* a tiny sailing boat built in Bangladesh.... Every day I have learned more about how to listen to the sea and my respect for the world's oceans has grown accordingly.

Tara Tari is a very small boat, with little space on board. I live simply — only essentials, what I really need. No gadgets, no unnecessary packaging, few clothes, and only one of each item.

"The Oceans represent our future, and as such we should care for them as we would a treasure or person that we love."

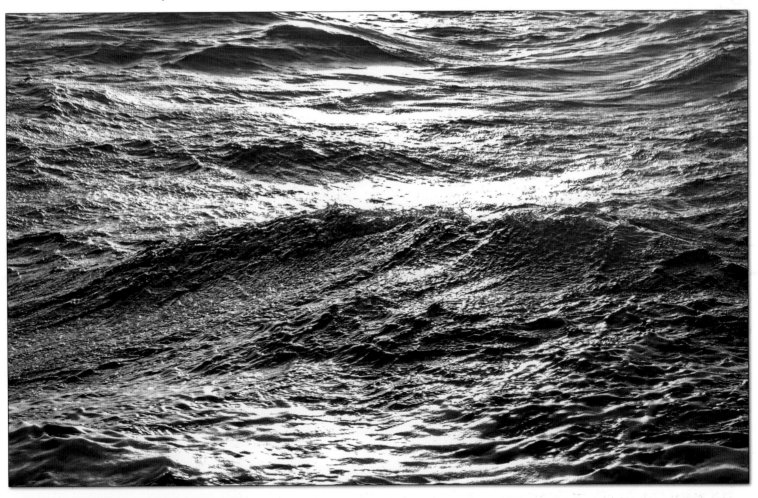

No television, no music — only a small number of books, a harmonica, and brushes for writing and drawing.

This adventure has taught me that we need very little to live well. If we focus on what we really need, we can reduce the amount of things in our lives and hopefully return to a more natural way of life, learning what nature can teach us: how to read the weather from cloud formations, the stars for orientation, the names of fish, plants, and flowers.

Tara Tari is my tiny planet and I look after my limited resources on board so that my adventure can continue, while also respecting the Oceans, for which I hold so much affection....

"Tara Tari is my tiny planet..."

More...

Have you ever encountered bad storms?

Storms have been the worst and also the best moments: the worst because you feel as a human, you're insignificant against the Ocean, but as sailor, you can't let fear take over. You have to act; you go with nature, rather than go against her.

How about wonderful moments at sea?

Strange forms approaching the hull of Tara Tari at high speed. The water is clear, the moon bright, these rippling silhouettes sparkle.

> **"Storms have been
> the worst and also
> the best moments . . ."**

Did shooting stars fall into the water? Sirens of the sea? Whatever these dolphins are dreaming, they come play with me; some jump from side to side, they splash me.

The boat is flying along. Out in front, others play with the bow wave. It's magical. *Tara Tari* is so low in the water that these magicians are a few inches from me. I go to the front, kneeling on the bow, and embrace the magic.

The dolphins smile. *"Merci la vie!"* I shout with joy, and plunge my arm into the water. The dolphins caress the tip of my hand, physical contact in this water so pure. "Thank you…" I say in a low voice, intoxicated by the spectacle, tears in my eyes.

I'm not crazy. The boat flies under the moon at night, the water so beautiful, it's almost too much magic to bear. I wish you could witness such moments. The truth is out there, in front of the bow. Open your eyes. Open your hearts. Look.

WhereIsTaraTari.blogspot.com

> *"Whatever these dolphins dream, they come play with me; some jump from side to side, they splash me."*

> *"This adventure has taught me that we need very little to live well."*

147

Sailing Solo on the High Seas

Sven in the '60s

Sven Yrvind

Late in 2012, my friend Bill Bullis mailed me a Wall Street Journal *article on a Swedish sailor planning to go around the world in a tiny (10´) sailboat. I looked up Sven Yrvind's website and found it loaded with photos and a practically book-length journal of his worldwide adventures.*

What fascinated me was the chunky little boat, which he plans to sail solo for 600 days, and which he claims can capsize or pitch pole and will still pop back upright. He plans to take everything he needs for two years' survival with him.

I've had a bunch of email and telephone correspondence with Sven, and finally talked him into writing a condensed (very condensed!) version of his adventurous life.

—LK

I WAS BORN ON THE windward side of a tiny island in the North Sea. Before, my family had lived in Stockholm, but the father of my great grandmother's grandmother, Jacob Johan Anckarström, killed Gustav III, the king, in 1792. Events following the murder forced our family to move to a more obscure environment.

My sister, my mother, my grandmother, my great grandmother, and I lived in a nice house 50 yards from the water. Women surrounded me. The male part of our family was at sea earning our upkeep. The day after Pearl Harbor was black in the family history; the British sank my father's ship in Hong Kong. To compensate, my grandmother gave me plenty of fish to eat in order that I could become strong enough to carry the family burden.

The next step in my education was going to school on the mainland to learn how to read and write. Unfortunately, the teacher diagnosed me as a problem child the very first day. My mother tried another approach and sent me to a boarding school, but after six years, they had not cured my dyslexia. Instead of getting a higher education, I found work as a mechanic.

At nineteen I was forced into military duty. From the very first day, it became apparent that we had different ideas about war. I was put behind bars. I escaped. The police hunted me. Six months later I was in a real prison.

There I was accused of starting a mutiny and transferred to solitary confinement in a high-security prison. I did not cooperate. Finally I was let out, but only after they had forced me to sign a paper stating that I was a psychopath.

In civil life, the psychopath certificate meant I couldn't get a job. However, beyond society's hidden rules and preconceptions, there is always a simple functional solution.

In 1962, I bought a 15´ open boat for the equivalent of $50, money they had given me to start a new life with. After I had added a deckhouse, I had my own tiny home.

With that little boat, I left Sweden on my own. It was not a long voyage, but it was a first step in a new successful lifestyle.

My time since then has been spent perfecting that way of life. First I learned mathematics; this took me three years. I was able to get teaching jobs, working with problem children.

Blekingeekan, a 15´ open boat that Sven bought for $50 in 1962. He added a deckhouse and two masts.

> ## "We tried to round Cape Horn, only to be capsized, and a week later, pitch-poled in a terrible storm."

With new money and knowledge, I decked a 14′ rowboat and sailed her to England in 1968. There I apprenticed at cold molding.

Back in Sweden, I then built a 20′ double-ender in my mother's basement in the early '70s.

With her and Janneke, a girl I had met in Holland, I sailed to Brazil and Argentina. We tried to round Cape Horn, only to be capsized, and a week later, pitch-poled in a terrible storm. But a small boat well-conceived is hard to kill.

> ## "But a small boat well-conceived is hard to kill."

More...

Blekingeekan, a 15′ open boat that Sven bought for $50 in 1962. He added a deckhouse and two masts.

In 1974, Sven built a 20′ double-ender, Bris, with one mast and a deckhouse on the stern.

"I designed a new boat in 1974, and headed east, running with the prevailing westerlies for Tristan da Cunha. . . ."

I designed a new boat in 1974, and headed east, running with the prevailing westerlies for Tristan da Cunha, a dot in the immensely big ocean; it is the world's most isolated island. It had 293 inhabitants, but no harbor. No matter, the citizens pulled her up on the beach, and I stayed there teaching mathematics for four months.

"I know that at sea, my sensory awareness increases and that takes me up to higher spiritual spheres."

We live in a world of over-stimulation. Stimulation from TV, computers, dopamine releasers, spiced food, and other drugs are reducing the size of our sense receptors. In contrast, I know that at sea, my sensory awareness increases, and that takes me up to higher spiritual spheres.

And what alternatives do I have, with my wretched monthly pension of 500 €? If I, like my fellow pensioners, bought a TV and a remote control with big buttons, and surfed the channels, I would get bored. I would lose my form; I would become fat and slow-witted, maybe get diabetes and have a stroke. Then they would put me in a long-stay hospital and connect me to a system of life-supporting machines. Chained to my bed, longing for the free horizons, I would suffer hell. I would spend my last decades trying to persuade someone to help me commit suicide.

No, TV is not for me. I must have something to live for, problems to solve.

Most people misunderstand life. Money does not make you happy. Comfort does not make you happy. On the contrary, comfort is dangerous to your health. It makes you lazy, fat, and bored. It is only by using energy that you create more energy, and it is that surplus of energy that makes you happy and healthy.

Sven's website: *www.yrvind.com*
Wall Street Journal article: *www.shltr.net/16Nws9k*

Above left, right, and below: Bris

"Most people misunderstand life. Money does not make you happy. Comfort does not make you happy."

Yrvind.com, 15′ long, 4′ wide; it is 4′ deep and has a draft of 12″. In 2011, Sven trailered it to Kinsale, Ireland, and set sail across the Bay of Biscay for Madeira, which he reached in 30 days. He then sailed to the Marquesas Islands (45 days), then shipped it in a container back to Sweden.

"It is only by using energy that you create more energy, and it is that surplus of energy that makes you happy and healthy."

Sven's Next Boat

After more than 50 years of designing building and sailing small crafts over big oceans to distant islands, I am now building a 10′ boat to circumnavigate the world nonstop — a 30,000 nautical mile voyage that will last 600 days without landing. I will carry 800 pounds of food and 200 pounds of books. I will drink rainwater.

When *CNN* and *The Wall Street Journal* wrote about my project, the most frequent comment was "suicide project." I beg to differ. A small boat, well-designed and built, is safer than a big one. The forces acting on it are smaller and it does not need complex machinery. To live among the waves is not to live in a war zone. It is life on land that is dangerous.

"I am now building a 10′ boat to circumnavigate the world nonstop — a 30,000 nautical mile voyage that will last 600 days without landing."

Drawing © 2013 by Olle Landsel for the Swedish yachting magazine Segling.

Living Aboard a Sailboat: A Way of Life

Teresa Carey

*We discovered Teresa in one of the excellent videos of tiny homes produced by Fair Companies of Barcelona (**www.shltr.net/thom-carey**). This is Kirsten Dirksen's introduction to the video:*

When Teresa Carey lost most of her possessions in a house fire years ago, she felt liberated. "I didn't miss a thing. It was almost like a burden lifted off my shoulders."

This was the first step toward a more minimalist lifestyle. The second motivating catalyst was her decision to life aboard her sailboat. Before making the move she began to downsize her stuff, keeping only what would fit in her car. When she finally made her move to her 27-foot sloop, she had given away or sold the majority of her belongings.

Today, Teresa lives on her sailboat Daphne with no flush toilet or shower, an icebox for a refrigerator, no television, and few electronics. She doesn't see it as a sacrifice, but as an opportunity to live a bigger life, unfettered by her possessions.

I PURCHASED MY NOR'SEA 27 and moved aboard in 2008. I went from living on a farm to living on the sea; from acres of land and room to roam, to a cabin space of about 100 square feet. But the benefits far exceed the limited space in my tiny boat.

The most important thing that living aboard a boat provides is not only a way to explore new places, but also the impulse to do so. Every day I wake up or return to a home that is mobile by design. It's built to go exploring and gives me a reason to challenge myself to go new places. The water beneath my hull connects me to every continent and a vast variety of cultures.

People often need a bigger house because from inside, they're always looking at the same scenery. A boat provides an endless variety of views, with constantly evolving surroundings. Each season brings not only new colors but a new way of life. Summer or southern climates make living aboard easy. The space expands from a tiny cabin cave to the entire deck, with walls the distant horizon.

But fall winds usher in the cold snowy winter. That's a time when I either sail south to escape the snow, or begin the work of preparing my boat to be most efficient and warm. During those dark months, I'm confined to *Daphne's* shrinking cabin. I pack the aft cabin with sails and seal off the lockers so there is less space to heat. I cover the entire boat with a large brown

"Teresa lives on her sailboat Daphne with no flush toilet or shower, an icebox for a refrigerator, no television, and few electronics."

"The water beneath my hull connects me to every continent and a vast variety of cultures."

canvas tarp that blocks any light from entering my ports.

But small living spaces also have their benefits. I am able to save money and enjoy life much more. *Daphne's* lockers are small, which limit my possessions. I have to carefully select what is most important to me, and find a balance between what I want and what will fit in the space I have.

I equipped *Daphne* with a single solar panel, which usually provides enough electricity to power my priority electronics: computer and lights. But the hair dryer never sees any use, and things like a microwave, stereo, television, and even a toaster are left ashore. As I monitor how much stuff crowds my life and how much energy I use, I've learned to appreciate, more than ever, all that I have.

Living on my boat allows me to develop a deep connection with the environment, which dares me to be adaptable, resilient, and simultaneously confident and unassuming with every challenge. During the times when others can shut the door on stormy weather, I'm more likely to be donning my foul weather gear and heading out into it. If I'm sailing, I might reef the sails or make sure things are lashed down. If I'm at anchor, I'll send out more anchor chain or simply sit in the cockpit to watch the boat and make sure the anchor holds fast. The rain will beat down the wind, blowing it in my face. And while I sit, I'll ignore the weariness that creeps in from staying up through the night. Even then, when I'm cold, wet, and tired, I know that despite living in a small space, I'm experiencing a life that is larger than myself.

 **www.TeresaCarey.com**

More...

The Nor'sea 27 is a 27′ fiberglass sloop. Her name is Daphne and she was made in 1991. All boats are female and referred to as a "she," even if they have a male name. That tradition dates back to times when women weren't allowed on a boat. She is 27′ long, but smaller than a typical 27′ boat in that her beam (width at the widest point) is only 8′. It's typically 10′ in a boat of that length. She is also considered a pock cruiser because of her size and a bluewater boat because of her seaworthiness. She is incredibly seaworthy. You could take her across the ocean. She is a heavy-displacement vessel, which means she is not a nimble racing boat, but designed instead to be rugged in rough ocean waters.

"During the times when others can shut the door on stormy weather, I'm more likely to be donning my foul weather gear and heading out into it."

"Living on my boat allows me to develop a deep connection with the environment..."

"When I'm cold, wet, and tired, I know that despite living in a small space, I'm experiencing a life that is larger than myself."

Misty Across the Pacific

> "After three years in Mexico, which included 15 months of hard work in a boatyard, Misty was ready for a new voyage: the South Pacific."

Henrick Lindström

Sailing toward Tonga

We published two pages on Swedish welder Henrick Lindström and his steel sailboat Misty in Tiny Homes (pp. 204–205). Here is the continuation of Henrick's, Ginni's, and Misty's voyage on the high seas.

AFTER THREE YEARS IN Mexico, which included 15 months of hard work in a boatyard, Misty was ready for a new voyage: the South Pacific.

She had undergone a major refit, including new bowsprit and aft platform with a solid railing between. Also kayak racks, a new engine bed, and changes in the interior. All metal surfaces on the hull were repainted and another thousand things were fixed.

Ginni and I loaded up Misty with 10 months of food: rice, beans, pasta, soy protein, cereal, dehydrated food, and canned

food; 200 liters of fresh water in the tank and our small water maker (desalinator) to produce more fresh water once we were under way.

We left Mexico from the tip of Baja California at the end of April and set sail toward French Polynesia. We crossed the equator and the doldrums

on the way. Periods of no wind alternated with heavy squalls. We motored through some parts of it. In the calm water we also did some kayaking and snorkeling; one day a school of dorados surrounded us with their brilliant colors.

Sailing to the Marquesas Islands took 25 days. Between rainstorms, the Marquesas' verdant pinnacles came to life with rainbows and white terns chasing each other in the sunlight. We spent five weeks there and visited three islands.

"Between rainstorms, the Marquesas' verdant pinnacles came to life with rainbows and white terns chasing each other in the sunlight."

Puerto Escondido, Mexico

Misty's trip, island by island:
Guaymas, Mexico / Cabo San Lucas, Baja California Sur, Mexico / Nuku Hiva, Marquesas, French Polynesia (FP) / Ua Huka, Marquesas, (FP) / Ua Pou, Marquesas, (FP) / Makemo Atoll, Tuamotus, (FP) / Fakarava atoll, Tuamotus, (FP) / Tahanea, Tuamotus, (FP) / Tahiti, Society Islands, (FP) / Moorea, Society Islands, (FP) / Raiatea, Society Islands, (FP) / Bora Bora, Society Islands, (FP) / Vava'u group, Tonga (north) / Haapia group Tonga (central) / Tongatapu group (south) / Opua (Bay of Islands), New Zealand

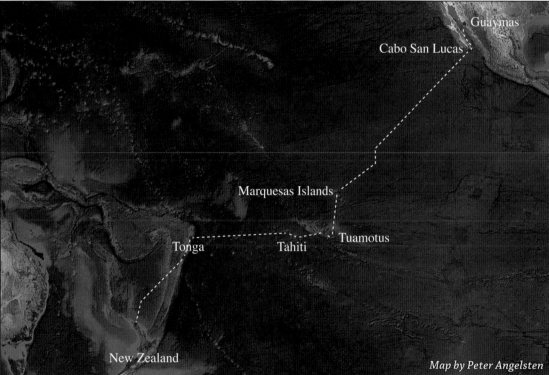

Guaymas
Cabo San Lucas
Marquesas Islands
Tuamotus
Tonga
Tahiti
New Zealand

Map by Peter Angelsten

More...

Misty at anchor, morning, Raiatea

Mountains, Ua Pou, Marquesas

Kayaks, palm trees on Motu

Kayak sailing, Makemo Atoll, Tuamotus

French Polynesia

A week after leaving the Marquesas, we reached Tuamotus, an archipelago of many atolls, spread out in a 1,000-mile area. To enter or exit an atoll can be exciting because of the strong tidal current. Traveling inside the lagoon requires good eyeball navigation with the best sunlight to avoid the minefield of coral heads. Atolls are rich with sea life. Sometimes we drifted about in our kayaks, leaning on each other's boats to put our snorkeled faces in the water and look around.

When the swell is up, water surges into an atoll over the reef and pours out through the passes. Snorkeling through eroded passages is like swimming in whitewater while watching a fish movie.

In Fakarava Atoll we scuba dived among dozens of reef sharks, manta rays, and lots of other tropical fish. Our technique for capturing wild coconuts improved with practice, and went from producing great laughter (or cursing) to providing food. We ate them fresh, drank the water inside, cooked with them, and filled one with rum.

Palm trees, Fakarava Atoll

Scuba diving, Fakarava Atoll

Beachcombing, Tuamotus

Frigate Bird, Tuamotus

Misty anchored in sunset, Tuamotus

Henrik in kayak, Bora Bora

Henrik with coconut, Tahanea Atoll

Outrigger in surf, Tahiti

Ginni in dingy, Tahanea Atoll, Tuamotus

We occasionally caught fish by line, spear, and a hand-held scoop net. Around the atolls, we got to see seabirds nesting in the tropical trees.

We left Makemo Atoll on an ebb, getting flushed out between standing waves on both sides. We spent 1½ months in the Tuamotus atolls, which proved to be our favorite place.

Next stop, Society Islands, and back to civilization. Tahiti, Moorea, Raiatea, and Bora-Bora had more people, boats, and vehicles. Also more elevation, variety, Internet access, baguettes, brie cheese, and friendly locals with overpowered motorboats willing to pull a stray sailboat off the reef.

"When the swell is up, water surges into an atoll over the reef and pours out through the passes. Snorkeling through eroded passages is like swimming in whitewater while watching a fish movie."

Flying fish, sailing toward Marquesas

Sunset, Moorea

*Remora fish under Misty,
Makemo Atoll, Tuamotus*

More...

Ginni kayak sailing, Tahiti-Moorea

Tonga

Between some of the islands I sailed single-handed and Ginni paddled and sailed her kayak. After another 1½ months, we left French Polynesia for Tonga. In 14 days we arrived in Tonga's Vava'u group, where coastlines of limestone cliffs are riddled with caves. Some you can paddle into and some you have to enter under water.

Kayak in limestone cave, Vava'u, Tonga

Shipwreck diving, Ha'afeva Island, Tonga (left, above, right)

Entering Bay of Islands, NZ after sailing from Tonga

Boats anchored, Bay of Islands, NZ

New Zealand

The infamous 1,000 nautical mile crossing to New Zealand needs a good weather window. When we left Tongatapu and sailed southwest, we knew bad weather was coming, but expected it to pass behind us. It did, by a few feet. When I put the mainsail back up after days of strong gales, floating pumice rocks fell out of the folds of the sail. Waves had lodged them there as they crashed over Misty's cabin top.

We made it to New Zealand, tired but thankful. Over the past seven months, our tiny floating home had carried us 6,800 nautical miles to some beautiful and remote places.

www.OnVoyage.net
KayakTravel.blogspot.com

A morning near Opua

"We made it to New Zealand, tired but thankful."

Cave paddling, Bay of Islands, NZ

Tolly's Sailboat
Iain Tolhurst

by Richard Ieian Jones

NAIDA WAS LAUNCHED IN THE summer of 2011. But her story starts back in 1987, when southern Britain was struck by a hurricane, which devastated our tree population. Swathes of ancient trees fell in the heavy winds. Tolly managed to salvage a lot of tree trunks and got them milled into boards — not quite knowing what he would do with them. But this was far too good a resource to waste on firewood.

The lumber sat for ten years, while Tolly decided what to build. At some point he bumped into Robin Knox Johnson, who advised him that a boat to be sailed single-handedly was best if pointed at both ends. After years of searching, Tolly discovered the "Pinky Ketch," a type of sailboat originally from the East Coast of the U.S.A.

Naida is a distinctly hand-built boat. Tolly can identify where every piece of wood stood as a tree within a 3-mile radius of the building site — the only exception being recycled deck timbers sawn from reclaimed factory beams.

It took a painstaking 12 years to build Naida — every evening and weekend and whenever there were a few hours when work allowed.

Tolly has focused determination unlike anyone I've ever met. To build a yacht is amazing in itself, but to do it from the the very woods that surround you is astounding in this day and age.

I recall standing in the galley admiring the sheer craftsmanship of the interior. Ash and yew, a surprising, but beautiful combination. Tolly told me the yew fell right there, pointing out of the porthole a few feet away. We had to move it out of the way when we brought the boat out of the shed. He thought it looked solid and planked it and it became this glorious interior.

Tolly is an organic grower, world-renowned for his growing techniques and ethos. He is vegetarian and refuses to use any animal manure on his crops. He believes in feeding the world organically and sustainably. He is a constantly busy man, rarely has the time to chat, as he's always doing something, trying to cram as

"Tolly managed to salvage a lot of tree trunks and got them milled into boards . . ."

"It took a painstaking 12 years to build Naida . . ."

much into his day as possible. He runs a local organic box scheme, bringing seasonal food to local families.

He has built five houses now, and still does not own one! He's living in the "cabin" (the shed that was built to make the boat in).

Originally he told me he was going to launch Naida quietly — midweek, while nobody was looking, in case anything went wrong. He didn't get away with this! It became an event. All those folks who had stopped to admire her during the build turned up, including the designer and the local kids lining the riverbanks.

She got craned out of the yard, over the trees, and onto the road. Slowly

> ## "He has built five houses now, and still does not own one! He is living in the 'cabin' (the shed that was built to make the boat in)."

she was edged the 400 yards down to the river Thames. A week later, people gathered, the band played, and there was a fly-by by two stunt planes! After a prayer giving thanks to the earth for her trees and minerals, and the breaking of a bottle of champagne, a huge crane lifted her out into the middle of the river, where it was deep enough for her to float.

The designer advised she would trim ½″ bow light, as her mast was not upright yet, and that there would be a leak — some cock left open or some jubilee clip not tightened.

She floated, ½″ high. Tolly zipped out in a launch, still looking tense. Bob, his friend and greatest helper, dived from the bank, swam out, and hauled himself aboard. No leaks. Thumbs up, applause all around.

She spent a few weeks traveling down the Thames to the sea, had some gearbox repairs, and re-trimming on the way, and now lies in Devon on the south coast.

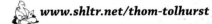 *www.shltr.net/thom-tolhurst*

More...

"She spent a few weeks traveling down the Thames to the sea, had some gearbox repairs, and re-trimming on the way. She now lies in Devon on the south coast."

The LunaSea
Luke Griswold-Tergis

I BOUGHT THE LUNASEA IN SOUTH San Francisco in 2005 for $1,000 from two Stanford physics grad students. She was a soggy ripped-apart mess, half sunk with 6″ of water over the floorboards. They had tried to renovate her to be a liveaboard and failed.

I spent a winter working on her, and my $1,000 boat quickly became way more expensive. In fact, for the amount of money I spent getting her functional, I could have just bought a working boat and gone sailing rather than boat repairing.

> *"Over the seven years I've had her, she has been an endless source of adventure . . ."*

In the beginning of summer, I loaded her on a trailer, hauled her up to Seattle, and with my friend and "anti-captain" Holly Gray, sailed her up the Inside Passage to Alaska.

Over the seven years I've had her, she has been an endless source of adventure (and a few terrifying experiences), carrying me to places in the islands and fjords of coastal Alaska and British Columbia few people have the chance to see.

She has been my floating shack in Haines, a convenient form of transportation, and a mobile documentary production studio.

She is a U.S. Yacht 27 built (according to some) for racing in 1983, to wit: she has a deep fin keel, a spade rudder, and a wide flat belly with a lot of beam. This means she is rather fast and responsive and at the same time has a lot of interior space. It also means she is not a very tough boat — speed and spaciousness being somewhat at odds with seaworthiness — so I wouldn't try to sail her to Hawaii, although one could probably survive the trip. (I know a dude who sailed a raft made of plastic bottles, fishnet, and the fuselage of a Cessna to Hawaii.)

' It took her awhile to transition from a California weekend racer to a pragmatic Alaskan boat. The first significant addition was a wood stove. I installed the stove in December during a cold snap when the harbor had pancake ice and the inside walls of LunaSea had grown about a half-inch of hoar frost. It was like living in a walk-in freezer. The wood stove solved that very quickly.

The next addition was a small house built over the hatch that allowed me to drive the boat sitting inside (with a fire going): warm, snug, and dry, sipping a cup of tea. Steering was accomplished via two strings run via pulleys to the wheel. I recently upgraded from the strings to an autopilot. I also painted her black and red. Anywhere in the world other than Alaska, this would be a horrible idea, but in Alaska, the extra heat is great. Open the hatches and let her dry out after a long rainy spell.

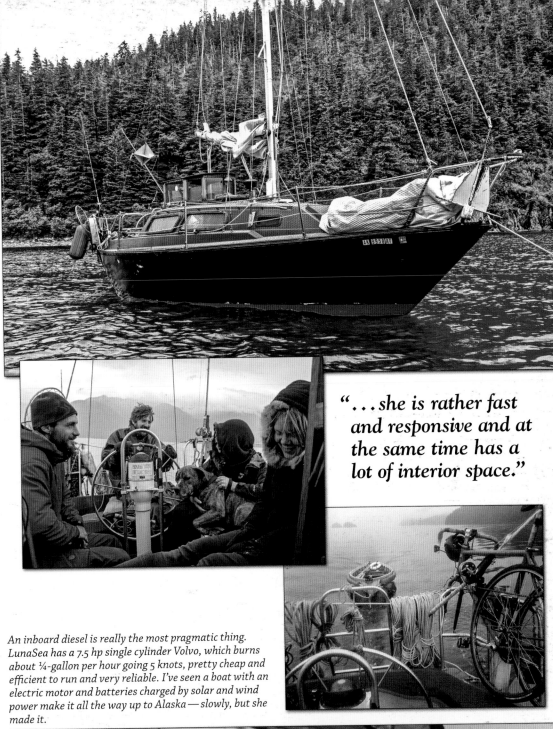

> "...she is rather fast and responsive and at the same time has a lot of interior space."

An inboard diesel is really the most pragmatic thing. LunaSea has a 7.5 hp single cylinder Volvo, which burns about ¼-gallon per hour going 5 knots, pretty cheap and efficient to run and very reliable. I've seen a boat with an electric motor and batteries charged by solar and wind power make it all the way up to Alaska — slowly, but she made it.

More...

In a place where the tides can range more than 20 feet, a shoal draft boat — or better yet, a boat that can easily be beached, a barge, catamaran, swing keel, or bilge keel boat — would offer a lot more versatility to explore river mouths, lagoons, small shallow bays, and estuaries, and to stay in these places. It would be nice to wake up in the morning and step off my boat into the grass, go for a walk, come back when the tide floats her and continue on my trip. The Yonder (see next two pages) has a centerboard so she can go lots of places the LunaSea can't.

The wind is finicky. On the fjords it will be dead against you or dead with you. Often there will be absolutely no wind and you motor, or if you are stubborn you row or drift with the tide when it goes your way. There is often way too much wind. Once the wind went from nothing to a 40-knot gale in about 5 minutes and I ended up with a broken mast.

'. . . carrying me to places in the islands and fjords of coastal Alaska and British Columbia few people have the chance to see. '

I sometimes wish I had a smaller boat. The problem with a liveaboard sailboat is that wherever I go, at the end of the day I am looking at the inside walls of the same plastic bucket. This is mighty comfortable and convenient but sometimes I think would have more fun if I had to drag my boat up on the beach, pitch a tent and build a fire and keep a lookout for bears. I would be much more present in whatever location I was at.

The Yonder
Luke Griswold-Tergis

THE YONDER IS JOEY JACOBSON'S sometime home, mobile ship-wright's toolbox, subsistence fishing boat, and primary transportation in a part of the world where fjords and straits are the only highways. He says, "She was the first thing that was my own really—a bedroom, an island at anchor."

He spends less time living on her these days as his entourage of dogs and children grows. Joey grew up in the midst of his father, Terry Jacobson's boat building project—the power scow Arcturas. Not surprisingly, he was a bit watercraft-obsessed as a child. His mother, Jenn Reid, banned the use of the word BOAT in the house.

The Yonder was built in 1933 as a Bristol Bay gill-netter. At the time manage-ment rules to limit fishing in Bristol Bay mandated that all fishing had to be conducted without a motor, under sail or via oar power. The Yonder has gone through many incarnations since she left Bristol Bay, and for the past couple of decades she has operated as a hand troller out of Port Alexander.

Joey got her from his friend Dean Pansano in Sitka and sailed her up to Haines. Along with his partner in crime, Merrick, and friends, he winched her up on the beach in front of his parents' house and built a boat shop over her out of driftwood, scrap lumber, tin, and tarps. She spent two years out of the water while Joey worked on her, rebuilding her decks, adding the house, and having wild mid-winter boat shop parties. More than once he woke up in the sawdust under the boat.

Joey says: "The Yonder has the simplicity we need to just get out of town." Most recently he added a Perkins diesel to replace the outboard, and this made the Yonder a lot more seaworthy.

Before the diesel, I was out with Joey on a rough day. When the boat pitched, the propeller came completely clear of the water, the engine racing, and then with the next wave, the motor was fully submerged. Nothing like a little salt water in the carburetor to slow you down. When it wouldn't start, we had to raise sail and tack through the rocks and around the point.

Maybe someday Joey's daughter, Yarona Blue Jacobson, will operate her as a hand troller, or in a future when petroleum is scarce and increasingly expensive, as a sailing gill netter.

"...primary transportation in a part of the world where fjords and straits are the only highways."

170

Fishing from the Yonder in light winds on Cross Sound. This day culminated with us picking the wrong route through the Inian Islands, nearly hitting a whale, getting sucked through Middle Pass by the tiderip, and nearly getting eaten by sea lions.

Joey Jacobson, Merrick Bochart, and Lauren McPhun sailing the Yonder through the high water pass in Swanson Harbor, a shortcut connecting Icy Strait with the Lyn Canal. There was a high probability of suddenly running aground at the moment this photo was taken, hence everybody but Joey is a little worried.

–Photo by Holly Gray

"The Yonder was built in 1933 as a Bristol Bay gill-netter."

Joey Jacobson, Merrick Bochart, and Lauren McPhun repairing the sail on the Yonder while leaving Auk Bay.

–Photo by Holly Gray

Joey Jacobson employs a tried and true "analog" depth sounder when navigating the Yonder in shallow water.

"She was the first thing that was my own really—
a bedroom, an island at anchor."

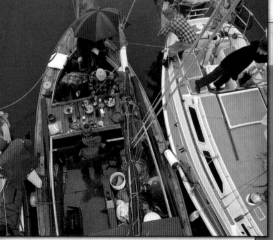

The Yonder (center) and two other boats rafted together for a group meal in Glacier Bay.
–Photo by Luke Griswold-Tergis

The Yonder running down Icy Strait in a west wind. Mt. Fairweather in the background
–Photo by Holly Gray

171

Native Girl
Rian Dickson and Jon Brown

"We had the good fortune of purchasing her in 2009 and have lived aboard since then."

RATHER THAN TELLING YOU THIS tale, I wish we could just have our old boat speak for herself. If these beams, frames, and planks could talk, they would tell you a very interesting story of which we, her current owners, are only a small part.

Launched in 1965 by the now locally famous Allen and Sharie Farrell, she is a beautiful example of what can be created from the materials that exist around us. Allen designed the boats and then they, as a couple, worked at phenomenal pace to put their vessels together. To the best of our knowledge,

Native Girl was constructed without power tools, which is in itself an incredible feat.

Allen's building style was a brilliant marriage of fish boat construction technique combined with an incredible eye for detail. So many aspects of their boats make you just stop and revel in how amazingly talented they were. During their lives together, the Farrells built six large sailboats and many smaller craft (all in British Columbia, Canada). Native Girl was built mostly of red cedar and is framed in yellow cedar. Originally rigged as a ketch, she is now a schooner with a yardarm to fly a square sail.

Upon completing Native Girl, the Farrells sailed to Mexico and Hawaii on two separate voyages, and made the boat their full-time home for over a decade. They actually owned the boat twice, having sold it once and then bought her back!

Since they sold Native Girl for the second time, she has switched hands a half dozen times and had many interesting owners. She has served as a home for well over half of her life on this coast. We had the good fortune of purchasing her in 2009 and have lived aboard since then. In many ways, it feels a privilege to be her current caretakers.

"...Native Girl was constructed without power tools..."

Vital Statistics

Length overall: 48 feet

Length on deck: 39 feet

Beam: 10´3˝

Construction: Strip-planked red cedar on yellow cedar frames

Rig: Schooner (originally a ketch, but converted by Allen and Sharie when they bought the boat back)

Built on Nelson Island, and launched in April 1965. It took 16 months from laying the keel to launching! With no power tools!

"...she is a beautiful example of what can be created from the materials that exist around us."

"Native Girl was built mostly of red cedar and is framed in yellow cedar."

"She has served as a home for well over half of her life on this coast."

ToomanyPocketts S./V.
Godfrey Stephens

MY LONG-TIME FRIEND Godfrey Stephens is a whirlwind of energy, enthusiasm and above all, art. He's contributed tremendously to our recent building books; much of the material in *Builders of the Pacific Coast* came directly or indirectly from him, including 10 pages on his carving, painting, and boats. There's also a full description of our friendship going back to 1964, so I won't repeat it here. There are a dozen pages in *Tiny Homes* from Godfrey's friends.

Godfrey's life has been so rich, so full, that it's just about impossible to document it. In addition to his art, he's been building and sailing boats for over 40 years. He had his first boat at age 12, an old dugout canoe that he sailed on a lake. "It just wired me to the water."

He built and sailed a 34′ Wharram catamaran around Vancouver Island in 1973. He built two lovely boats that he bequeathed to his daughters. (*See following four pages.*) He's sailed extensively in British Columbia and Washington, and made two trips to Mexico: the first time, in 1982, he got grounded off the coast of Baja California, but was able to get back out to sea; the

second time, in 1989, he ended up in a shipwreck—a total loss. All in all he's had 15-20 boats.

His latest sailboat is this little 12′ San Francisco Bay Pelican, a model designed in 1959 by Bill Short. It's a much-beloved boat among sailors.

Godfrey worked on and off for maybe a year customizing it. A leeboard on the side provides lateral resistance; this way he doesn't need a centerboard, and can go up on the beach. (It draws only 4″.) There's a Lexan skylight plus an extended tiller so he can stay dry while sailing in the rain. A tiny stove, sleeping space aboard. Minimal.

www.GodfreysArt.com

"His latest sailboat is this little 12′ San Francisco Bay Pelican . . ."

"A tiny stove, sleeping space aboard. Minimal."

Godfrey's boat, the Mungo, ran aground in Mexico in 1982, but he was able to get it off the beach and back to sea.

"... *can go up on the beach. (It draws only 4″.)*"

175

Chu Wey
Aija Steele

Over the years, Godfrey Stephens (see previous two pages) has given a handcrafted sailboat to each of his two daughters, Aija and Tilikum. Aija (now living on Salt Spring Island, BC) describes her boat here, and Tilikum does the same on the following two pages.

—LK

GODFREY FOUND THE derelict Saint Pierre et Miquelon (islands off Newfoundland) dory hull in the early 90s and converted it into a Chinese junk-rigged schooner, steel-sheathed, with twin bilge keels.

It is 27′ long and Godfrey named her Chu Wey (which means "See you, friend" in Nuu-chah-nulth). The rig was designed by the late Allen Farrell, legendary boat builder of British Columbia (whose boats included China Cloud and Native Girl).

The keels allow the sailboat to land on the beach and stay upright as the tide goes out. You can jump off and pick mussels, dig clams, or forage for berries. Shallow draught enables the boat to go places not many can. It's ideal for gunk holing and cruising right on past those busy anchorages, and landing on your own little patch of beach.

I lived aboard Chu Wey on and off for about 10 years, some of which was spent in the inter-tidal zone of Tofino Harbor. It was neat. Up and down with the tide, and taking off and landing throughout the night made for wild dreams.

Plus the little underwater window was right there by my pillow, so I could see the crabs scurrying about and seaweed floating by.

The wood stove is an essential part of ocean living, since things can get damp quickly in a temperate climate. A friend welded up an efficient, airtight stove for me out of a 10″ steel pipe and other recycled parts. Beachcombing for fir bark driftwood or "sea biscuits" to feed the stove was a huge part

"Up and down with the tide, and taking off and landing throughout the night made for wild dreams."

"I lived aboard Chu Wey on and off for about 10 years . . ."

of living onboard Chu Wey; the wood stove was also used for cooking.

Godfrey gave me the boat in 1997 just after I finished university and was deciding what to do next. He had just launched his sailboat Snookwis. We rafted both boats together and lived on them at Goose Spit in Comox.

After a couple of months, I sailed north to Sointula, Malcolm Island, which is at the northeast tip of Vancouver Island. Godfrey followed three weeks later on Snookwis, and we had a fabulous time hanging out with our Viking friends.

I ended up staying the winter, and the following summer made my way to Tofino on the west coast of Vancouver Island.

In 2002, after making new junk sails from crosshatched tarps, a friend and I sailed her down the west coast of Vancouver Island to East Sooke, just north of Victoria. What a trip! Socked-in fog while surfing wing-on-wing into Juan de Fuca Strait. Never a dull moment.

Chu Wey and I made Murder Bay (near Sooke) our home for the next few years, rowing out to sleep with the gentle swell of the Pacific in that quiet and wild place.

In 2005 we sailed her to Salt Spring Island where she is today, awaiting the next adventure!

"The keels allow the sailboat to land on the beach and stay upright as the tide goes out. You can jump off and pick mussels, dig clams, or forage for berries."

Snookwis
Tilikum Redding

ABOUT 36 YEARS AGO, my father, Godfrey Stephens, and his friend Jennifer found a water-logged red cedar dugout canoe surrounded by nettles, a home to frog spawn and algae; it's believed to have come from Nitinat on Vancouver Island, Canada.

Jennifer and Snookwis, 1979

> "*Godfrey Stephens and his friend Jennifer found a waterlogged red cedar dugout canoe . . .*"

Godfrey, being gifted with creative, artistic, and wild inspiration and an obsession with small, shallow draft boats (so he can get into shallow waters that others with deep keels can only dream of), saw beyond her sorry state and ended up in negotiations with the guys at Granville Island Marina. Godfrey carved a wooden sign for the marina and gave them $500. Doing so, he acquired the sad canoe, named her Snookwis, and soon dove into a labor of inspiration and passion (as most of Godfreys works of art are created). She was turned into a beautiful, functional, floating, and sailing creation of Godfrey's — organic abstract art with a cabin, mast, and sails — the makings of an able mini-cruising vessel.

Godfrey built many boats over the years, but he was never one to settle for any stage of a finished boat. Every time he returned to Snookwis, he'd set to work with renewed inspiration, and she morphed into many forms over the years.

In 1989 Snookwis provided a home for Godfrey after he was shipwrecked off the coast of Mexico. He had many memorable adventures in Snookwis throughout the Salish Sea and beyond.

> "*She was turned into a beautiful, functional, floating, and sailing creation of Godfrey's — organic abstract art with a cabin, mast, and sails . . .*"

> *"Tied to a kelp bed, fire burning in the little wood stove, the smell of cedar, pine tar, and salt, the sound of water against the ancient adzed and copper-sheathed hull with the moonlight shining in . . ."*

I was grateful to have been given Snookwis about 15 years ago. Godfrey's energy and attention were focused on building his 39′ steel sailboat, Mungo Nuevo, and Snookwis had fallen into a sorry state, so I sailed her away. My first night aboard was one of absolute contentment. Tied to a kelp bed, fire burning in the little wood stove, the smell of cedar, pine tar, and salt, the sound of water against the ancient adzed and copper-sheathed hull with the moonlight shining in. In the morning, little fish would jump, sounding like raindrops on the water. Looking through the underwater window, the mouths of small worm-like creatures were busy cleaning the glass.

My favorite of all journeys with Snookwis was crossing the Strait of Juan de Fuca after living for a summer at anchor in Mud Bay on San Juan Island, where I did volunteer work at the Center for Whale Research. About two hours out and a couple miles from shore, I was surrounded by seven orcas, all much bigger than Snookwis. They rolled, showing their bellies and spy-hopping, each movement causing Snookwis to rock & roll. It was a lovely 10 or so minutes shared sitting inside an ancient tree, looking through the underwater porthole at these magnificent creatures.

Snookwis is one of the simplest of homes, yet she transcends genres in her organic fantastical form and is appreciated by all who meet her. I've been told by many that she is in their top five boats of all time, sharing the spotlight with racing multihulls as well as wooden classics. Children love her and liken her to stories of fantastic imaginings.

She is more personality than object or thing. She is home and character, history, art, and a connection to another time that I wish for all to feel connected to.

Photo: Bob Sanderson

> *"In the morning, little fish would jump, sounding like raindrops on the water."*

Guided by the Stars, Powered by the Wind

More…

"The canoes have fiberglass catamaran hulls 72´ long by 21´ wide; each has a solar electric drive train with two 10 kW retractable podded drives and 135 sq. ft. of solar cells."

In Bolinas Bay

Pacific Voyagers

Photos by Greg Marcotte

I LIVE IN A SMALL TOWN on the Northern California coast and there's a bay where fishing boats sometimes seek shelter from the north winds.

In the early summer of 2011, local fisherman Greg Marcotte was heading out the channel in his boat to go abalone diving when he saw three large and unusual sailboats in the bay.

They turned out to be traditional Polynesian *vaka moana,* or oceangoing voyaging canoes, on a trip that had started in New Zealand, then went on to Tahiti, the Marquesas, Hawaii, and now were headed for San Francisco.

The ships are part of a six-canoe fleet called Pacific Voyagers, and their mission is to

"…use the wisdom of our ancestors, combined with modern science, to propel us into a more sustainable future, help heal our injured ocean, raise awareness, and to revive our cultural traditions of voyaging."

The canoes have fiberglass catamaran hulls 72´ long by 21´ wide; each has a solar electric drive train with two 10 kW retractable podded drives and 135 sq. ft. of solar cells.

Greg said that they navigated by star maps placed on the rails. The sailors knew the motions of specific stars — where they would rise and set on the horizon — and that they'd sit in a chair and line up the stars with the maps. "When you leave New Zealand, line up with the

Tahiti star…" and you'll go straight to Tahiti. (Polynesian navigation knowledge is passed along by oral tradition from navigator to apprentice, often in the form of song.)

Greg and his two young sons went out to the boats bearing fresh abalone and home-smoked salmon and hung out with the crew on several occasions. Some other local fishermen took them some halibut and ice cream. After a few days in the bay (a thrill to see!), the *vaka moana* headed for San Francisco.

On these two pages are Greg's photos of them here and on their trip into San Francisco, and the following two pages show the boats in various places in the Pacific Ocean.

"In the early summer of 2011, local fisherman Greg Marcotte was heading out the channel in his boat to go abalone diving when he saw three large and unusual sailboats in the bay."

Left and above: Boats anchored in Bolinas Bay

Left and above: Boats at Treasure Island

"Greg and his two young sons went out to the boats bearing fresh abalone and home-smoked salmon..."

"They turned out to be traditional Polynesian vaka moana, or oceangoing voyaging canoes..."

Eli at Treasure Island

Top right: Kingston, Simon, and Eli jumping off one of the boats at Treasure Island

Bottom right: Eli jumping near the Bay Bridge

More...

Guided by the stars, powered by the wind; the Pacific Ocean is our breath.

Photos by Rui Camilo, courtesy of Okeanos

We feel honored to continue in the wake of our ancestors, learning from their ancient wisdom, and venturing forth into the future with a new mission of healing our ocean and a rejuvenated Te Mana 'o Te Moana, *the Spirit of the Sea. Our Polynesian ancestors respected and cared for the sea. Like our forefathers, thousands of years before us, we travel using traditional* vaka moana — *ocean-going voyaging canoes. Our mission is simple: Use the wisdom of our ancestors, combined with modern science, to propel us into a more sustainable future, help heal our injured ocean, raise awareness, and to revive our cultural traditions of voyaging.*

—*Pacific Voyagers Foundation*

www.pacificvoyagers.org
www.navaldc.com/vaka_moana.html

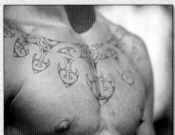

Solomon Islands

Fiji Islands

Polynesian navigation knowledge is passed along by oral tradition from navigator to apprentice, often in the form of song.

The Proa Jzerro

Russell Brown

"In 2000, my buddy Steve Callahan and I crossed the Pacific from San Francisco to the Marquesas Islands."

THE PROA IS AN INTRIGUING AND ancient sailboat concept that captured my imagination at a young age and never let go. I built my first one in the late '70s and sailed it to the Caribbean. I had enough crazy and cosmic experiences in the few years that I was on that boat to write a book about, but it was a tiny and very wet boat, so I built a bigger one.

I'm on my fourth proa now and it's still too small (36 feet in length), but I did get to do a big trip in it. In 2000, my buddy Steve Callahan and I crossed the Pacific from San Francisco to the Marquesas Islands. This was a passage that Steve and I both think of as our best adventure yet. I continued on to Australia, mostly by myself, stopping everywhere that I could along the way.

The following year I cruised the east coast of Australia and crossed to New Zealand before shipping the boat home in a container. I returned home to work on my career, which didn't turn out to be the best move, but I still have the boat, and maybe we'll go again.

Why a proa? Well, it's a brilliant concept. It was dreamed up by ancient Micronesians who didn't have great materials to work with, but did have a desire to colonize the Pacific, which meant sailing long distances against the wind.

At first glance, a proa looks lopsided or asymmetrical, but it's not. Most boats, vehicles,

and even creatures are symmetrical (or mirror-imaged) from side to side, but not from end to end. The proa is symmetrical from end to end, but not from side to side. The proa reverses directions when it tacks and always keeps the same side facing the wind; this is why it needs only one outrigger.

In modern times the proa has not been developed as have catamarans and trimarans, but that may have more to do with the human mind not being able to accept lateral asymmetry, because as a sailing concept, for both racing and cruising, the proa has a lot going for it.

My current proa Jzerro, shown in these photos, has turned out to be a pretty amazing boat. It has been a great little home for extended parts of my life, and a long-legged home when it comes to traveling.

PacificProa.net is a website with lots of stories, photos, and video. *Proafile.com* is a forum for developing designs and ideas. My website is: *PTWatercraft.com*, but I don't sell designs for proas and I much prefer sailing them to talking about them.

www.PacificProa.net
www.ProaFile.com
www.PTWatercraft.com
info@PTWatercraft.com

"At first glance, a proa looks lopsided or asymmetrical, but it's not."

"The proa reverses directions
when it tacks and
always keeps the same
side facing the wind . . ."

"It has been a great little home
for extended parts of my
life, and a long-legged home
when it comes to traveling."

Living Simply on a Sailboat

Brooks B. Whitehead

I LEAD A DELIBERATELY SIMPLE, DEEPLY casual life aboard my sailboat moored in Lake Union, a lake in the center of Seattle. It is a life I have chosen, which allows me tremendous freedom by living simply and living within my footprint. I am as close to living off the grid in the city as one can get, and best of all, my home is completely portable.

Living aboard a sailboat allows me the simplicity to focus on bigger-picture issues — the things I really need to think about, and not get caught up in culture of consumerism. As Henry David Thoreau wrote, "As you simplify your life, the laws of the universe will be simpler." As I once said, "We are the odd ones: The artists, bohemians, the free-thinkers. We choose to live on the water in unique shelters because we aren't afraid to be a little weird."

 *jackstub.blogspot.com*

"*I am as close to living off the grid in the city as one can get, and best of all, my home is completely portable.*"

"As you simplify your life, the laws of the universe will be simpler." –Henry David Thoreau

"It is a life I have chosen, which allows me tremendous freedom by living simply and living within my footprint."

Slider, a Cruising Catamaran
Ray Aldridge

LOYD, YOU MIGHT FIND THIS interesting for your new book. A few years ago I designed this little boat, and as far as I know, she's the only one like it in the world. She's a tiny catamaran, just 16 feet long, but has comfortable seating inside the hulls, so you can go cruising without having to squat on a trampoline, as with a beach cat. She's not nearly as fast as a beach cat, but faster than any 16-foot monohull cruiser.

One of the big reasons I drew the boat in the first place was to have an entry-level multihull for cruising that I could afford—and to me "cruising" implies overnighting, because if you don't stay out, you're just day sailing.

Slider is named after the Red-Eared Slider, a "...deceptively fast aquatic reptile."

She has an old-fashioned rig, a sprit sloop, chosen partly because it allows folks to make their own cheap mainsail out of polytarp and still get good performance. She is an open boat, but like many other open boats, you can overnight on her. I've stayed out for a week at a time. If the weather is nice, I just set up a folding cot on the center deck (if I'm alone) or a queen-sized air mattress if I'm with my wife.

It's really not practical to overnight with more than two aboard, but I have gone out for weekends with my two sons. We set up a shore tent on the beach. Here along the Gulf Coast, as in so many other places, often

Ray's sons by the campfire, during a weekend trip down Santa Rosa Sound, on the north Florida coast

Early morning near Pensacola Pass. The boom, sprit, and mainsail can be hauled up the mast to give standing headroom on the center deck.

there is no public land ashore for pitching a tent, so I have a pop tent for use on those occasions. It covers the center deck and one of the cockpits, which gives us a place to sit inside if the weather is bad.

One of the great things about Slider is that the two seats are movable, so that one person can sit facing forward to steer, using the steering lines that circle the deck on both sides, and the other can turn the other seat around and face aft to watch the fishing lines or the sunset.

Slider is trailerable without permits, being only 8'6" wide, and is sailed at that width, so launching her is about as complicated as launching a johnboat. Her mast is raised and secured with a non-stretch Dyneema lanyard, and takes only a couple of minutes to put up.

Steering is like sitting in an armchair, with the steering line running along your forearm on the side deck. It's the most comfortable steering setup I've ever seen; you can see where you're going and there's no twisting around to handle the tiller.

I really love that little boat. I've owned a lot of sailboats over the last 35 years, from large cruising yachts to tiny dinghies, but Slider is far and away my favorite of all.

I've sold quite a few plans, and sister ships are now sailing in many countries around the world. My website is: **www.shltr.net/thom-aldridge1**

I've also published a couple of pieces about her in *Small Craft Advisor*, and here's a link to a SCA blog post: **www.shltr.net/thom-aldridge2**

Inside one of the hulls of a larger cat I'm building now

Slider in a friend's slip, with a canopy and pop tent

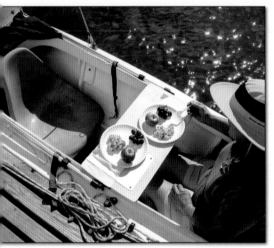

Picnic aboard Slider, showing the flexible seating and the cockpit table, which can also hold a one-burner stove for cooking under way

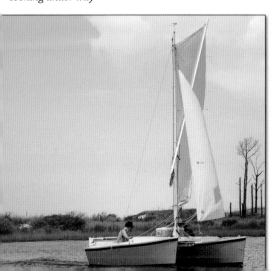

Perdido Key at sunset, looking south toward the Gulf

Sailboat on the Road
Kees Prins

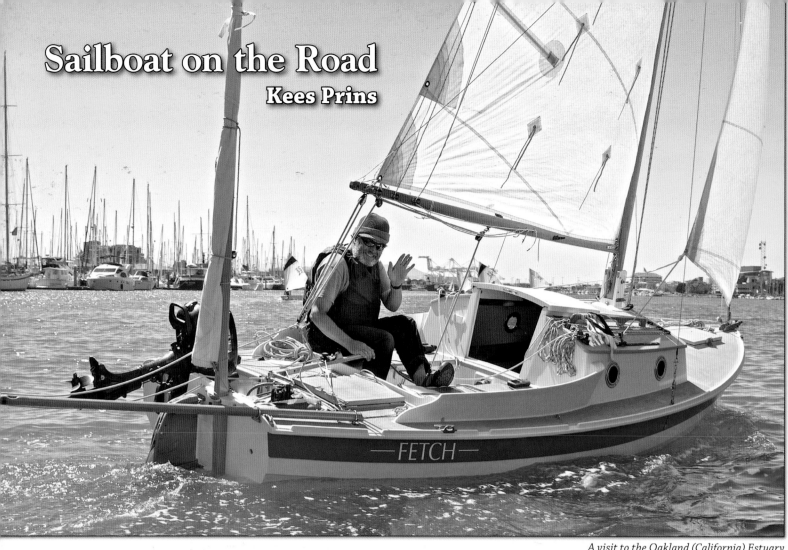

A visit to the Oakland (California) Estuary

AFTER A NICE SAIL WITH A FEW other small boat owners in the Oakland Estuary, I started on my journey across the country toward Maine. I didn't want to plan how I'd get there, but instead let things unfold.

It was a hot summer, so I took a more northerly route. It would not only be more comfortable for me, but also for my Dodge camper van pulling my sailboat Fetch behind.

Fetch is 17′ long, weighs 1,200 pounds, and has a minimal interior; I can sit up comfortably, lie down at night, and there's plenty of room for gear and food.

The van is quite heavy, about 7,800 pounds, so altogether quite a bit of weight to pull over mountain passes and such. It's great to have the van though, because I can stand up in it; it has a toilet, a small kitchen, a refrigerator, a heater, and air-conditioning.

Two years prior to this trip, I had bought Fetch as an open daysailer and decided to put decks and a cabin on her. It took about 600 hours to do the conversion in my free time. Now I had a boat I could cruise in, a pocket cruiser as they call it. All I needed next was time to use her.

After sailing her one season from my hometown, Port Townsend (Washington, USA), I started thinking about a more

"Fetch is 17′ long, weighs 1,200 pounds, and has a minimal interior; I can sit up comfortably, lie down at night, and there's plenty room for gear and food."

"It's great to have the van though, because I can stand up in it; it has a toilet, a small kitchen, a refrigerator, a heater, and air-conditioning."

substantial journey. I read a book about somebody cruising the Inner Coastal Way from Florida to New York and that area seemed appealing for a journey with Fetch.

My wife and I had just separated, the house was sold, and the kids were more or less grown up. I gave notice to the boat yard I was working for, bought a used camper van and off I went, for an indefinite amount of time.

In driving across the country I had stopped by Great Salt Lake for a few days. During a party in the marina, somebody recommended Jackson Lake, next to the Grand Tetons, so that's where I was heading next. The lake is indeed beautifully situated at the base of the gorgeous Grand Tetons, and soon I was sailing toward some islands under blue skies and a nice breeze.

After pulling into a stunning little cove, I met some folks camping out and promptly they invited me over for dinner. I spent a whole day with them, taking hikes and watching the full moon rise before I sailed off again. All the way along this trip I was running into people offering me places to stay and a chair at their dinner table; this trip was working out just fine.

Beached in a beautiful quiet cove on Elk Island, Jackson Lake, Wyoming

"The lake is indeed beautifully situated
at the base of the gorgeous Grand Tetons,
and soon I was sailing toward some
islands under blue skies and a nice breeze."

Sunrise while moon is setting over the Grand Tetons, Wyoming

193

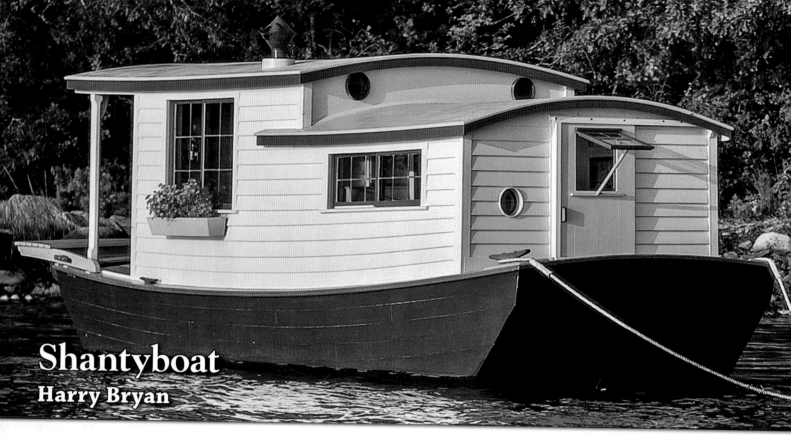

Shantyboat
Harry Bryan

Photos by Bryan Gagner

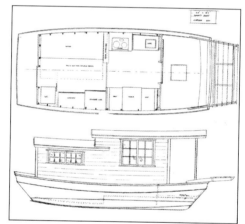

THE CONSTRUCTION OF OUR shantyboat could have been simpler if we had no rocker in the bottom and no curve in both the profile and plan views of the sheer. The house, too, might have been a box with right-angle corners. We chose to include subtle curves in the project both for increased efficiency moving through the water and to coax a smile from those who watch her swinging at the mooring. We were rewarded in an unexpected way by introducing a subtle sheer in the eave of the house top. The low point of this curve in the aft roofline directs the runoff from the evening dew directly into the window boxes, reducing the maintenance of the nasturtiums to a minimum.

There is no plywood in this boat, yet building her with that material would certainly have been an option. We chose natural wood because we are lucky enough to be able to get it and we believe that it imparts

"The low point of this curve in the aft roofline directs the runoff from the evening dew directly into the window boxes . . ."

a subtle yet appealing texture and feel to the project, which can be lost with engineered materials.

The hull is built upside down over ⅞″× 2″ oak frames set at each station. The bottom is epoxy laminated from two layers of ⅝″ cedar laid athwartships at 60 degrees to each other. Sides are ⅞″ cedar of carvel construction. Seams are caulked with cotton except that the garboard is edge-glued to the plank above. Thus, all seams below the waterline are glued, ensuring a tight hull.

House framing is spruce with the studs bolted to the sheer clamp as well as to a riser running below and parallel to the clamp. What appear to be clapboards are perhaps more correctly called lapstrake siding, as they are not tapered in section, as clapboard would be. The laps are fastened together and form the interior surface as well. In order to present a pleasing appearance, the siding is lined off, as would be the planks of a hull. This gives a smooth transition from the

"There is no plywood in this boat..."

curve of the sheer to the more subtle curve of the roof.

Decks and housetops are splined cedar covered with canvas laid in outdoor carpet cement and saturated in epoxy.

I feel that dividing the windows into multiple panes is an important part of the overall look of the boat. We chose to set them in lead cames (slender lead bars) because they obstruct the view less than heavier wood dividers. We also found leaded windows significantly easier to build in a shop with no specialized sash-making equipment.

———

The price of our shantyboat, including a wheelbarrow pram, was $75,000.

The owner of this first boat moors it off his wooded waterfront where it serves as a floating retreat. He has often entertained dinner guests who are either ferried from shore by dinghy or arrive in their own boats. The owner's wife has hosted afternoon Scrabble games with her friends.

For shantyboaters who choose to live aboard for some period of time, it may be wise to consider the development of a shantyboat ethic to avoid being seen as a non-taxpaying squatter by those fortunate enough to command an unspoiled view of the water. Loud parties, the use of private land for access without permission, or the dumping of waste of any kind should be high on the list of practices to avoid. Shifting moorings every two or three days will help to allay any worries of a sensitive landowner. Fortunately, the advantages of shallow draft and self-contained living open up count-less secluded anchorages unavailable to the average cruising boat.

Headroom in the forward section of the boat is 6´. Aft section is 6´4˝.

This is based on an article that appeared in Woodenboat *Magazine:* **www.woodenboat.com**.

Plans for the boat are available: **harrymartha@hotmail.com**.

The settee to starboard can be pulled out to convert to a double bed.

"We chose to include subtle curves in the project both for increased efficiency moving through the water and to coax a smile from those who watch her swinging at the mooring."

The windows have true divided lights.... This sliding door opens onto the shantyboat's "front porch."

Leviathan
Simon Birtwhistle

"Leviathan started life over 100 years ago as a coal-carrying butty (a barge with no engine)."

L EVIATHAN STARTED LIFE over 100 years ago as a coal-carrying butty (a barge with no engine). She had an elm bottom with the rest of the hull constructed in metal up to the gunwales. I was commissioned by her owner, Allen Acaster, to design and build an innovative interior and roof for this antique hull. So together we set about rebuilding her. Our mantra was "We must not go mental." Unfortunately we ignored ourselves and did just that.

We wanted to give the boat a surprise element, a feeling of "whatever next." So the exterior, quite dark and forlorn, was as traditional as could be with its black canvas roof and grey rear cabin.

Upon entering the craft, one is assaulted with a very different story. You enter by a most peculiar room, which throws the senses. A white bathroom perfectly proportioned and formed, the only colour a red potbelly stove and red rear

cabin doors. Beyond the room of white a very different scenario is encountered. Again, a low-ceiling affair, but this section is mainly black with a grey lump of metal sitting in the centre of the space. The walls and floor are adorned with industrial checker plate and neat lines of coloured wiring.

At the far end, a semicircular portal beckons one on to the greatest surprise of all. From the darkness and squareness of the engine room, one emerges into a cavernous space of light and curve. To achieve the lightness, we used American White Ash as the bulk of timber— which we cut, carved, and shaped with routers and angle grinders. The insulation was of the itchy fibre variety, and together with red and white leatherette, we ingeniously upholstered the sides, walls, and sloping ceilings. This gave it an industrial, plush asylum look.

All in all, we did go mental, and we would do it again at the drop of a hat.

www.SimonBirtwistle.co.uk

"We wanted to give the boat a surprise element, a feeling of 'whatever next.'"

"From the darkness and
squareness of the engine room,
one emerges into a cavernous
space of light and curve."

Houseboat in Southern England
Muriel Chvatal

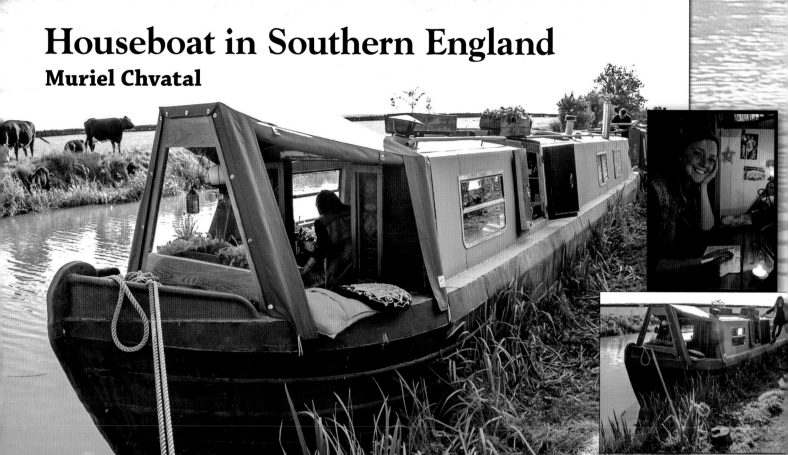

> *"Bijou, my 45-foot steely lady, and I have been floating on the still waters of the Kennet and Avon Canal for the past three winters."*

Kids born aboard

BIJOU, MY 45-FOOT STEELY LADY, and I have been floating on the still waters of the Kennet and Avon Canal for the past three winters. I am currently moored in a beautiful spot in Wiltshire, home to the ancient sacred sites of Avebury, Stonehenge, and the Westbury White Horse. I potter between two counties — a short distance considering that the waterways can take you to Liverpool, Leicester or London — all via the most picturesque rural routes.

Boat dwelling is the acceptable, if somewhat romanticized, face of nomadic living in the British countryside. The canals were originally constructed as transportation routes, with horse-drawn barges carrying cargoes such as coal, grain, and manufactured goods. Then the ascendancy of rail and road transport sent them into chronic decline.

The last half-century has seen the revival of the inland waterways as a leisure resource for those now living or holidaying on the water, as well as the cyclists, ramblers, and

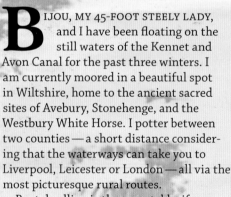

anglers using the towpaths running alongside. The gentle pace that previously allowed pottery to be transported without breaking is now a seductive and sought-after aspect of life on the canals.

I've become interested in what draws humans to water. Perhaps it is a cellular memory of our times as sea-dwelling creatures or our more recent experience in our mother's womb. Living on water can be a choice to return to basics — a self-imposed retreat to the source.

My own journey with Bijou started with the desire to build a nest, connect with a more natural order, and simplify my life. Leaving behind the noise of the city, I rediscovered the music of the land — and the water. Boaters live on close terms with

Nature—its changing weather, seasons, and wild things—herons, kingfishers, cormorants, water voles, a very occasional otter, and of course, the ever-present ducks.

My dream of simplicity soon gave way to hard work of a different nature, which comes with the lack of mod cons such as a fridge, central heating, a washing machine, or a car. An 80-watt solar panel covers most of my electricity needs in the summer. Launderettes are a different matter.

Living on a barge has been compared to living in a corridor. I have had to become selective about the height of my visitors! A narrowboat interior is typically just over six feet across and a little over that in height, though these figures might be more generous on modern models.

Living in a tiny home requires a certain creativity when it comes to the use of space and none is wasted here. A lot of the original fittings came out when I redesigned a more space-conscious layout and improved the insulation. Working alongside my carpenter friend, Jesus (really!) sharpened my DIY skills. The twice-collapsible sofa bed I built from scratch is my proudest creation. One common characteristic of a 'boatie' would be that of a contortionist with a can-do attitude and an affinity with water.

Folk that live afloat, like their vessels, come in all shapes and sizes: singletons, families (some with kids born on board), young or retired couples, and those just wishing to stay under the radar. Boaters form a strong mutual support network—albeit a largely transitory and widely dispersed one—readily sharing skills and looking out for one another. The local floating community has its own festival, outdoor cinema, shanty choir, and even a naked calendar! (Sorry, out of print.)

"Living on water can be a choice to return to basics—a self-imposed retreat to the source."

199

Houseboat in British Columbia

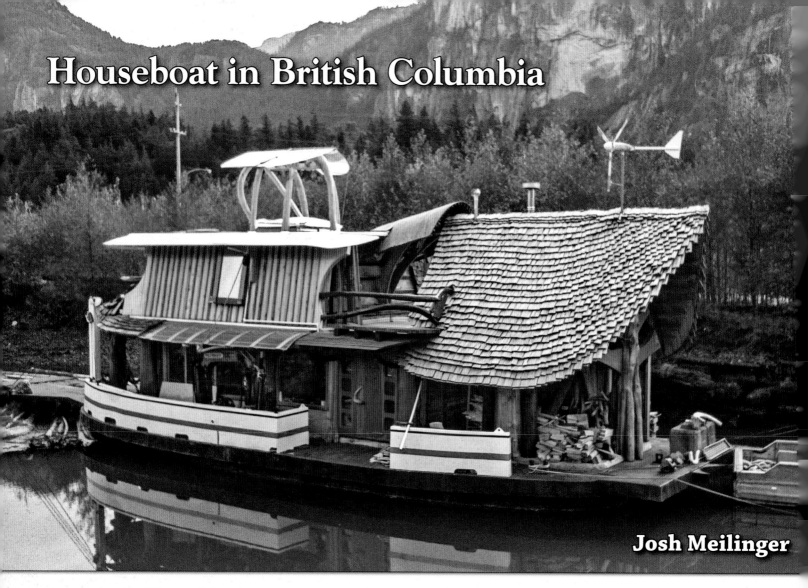

Josh Meilinger

> *"I would salvage an entire log, literally dragging it down the road with my 10′ trailer, milling everything with my Alaskan mill."*

Psalm 127:1: "Unless the Lord builds the house, its builders labor in vain."

I'M VERY THANKFUL FOR THE PATH I'VE been led on during this project and where it's taken me. All of the interesting people I've met, new arrivals (my baby girl, Julia), life's challenges that my wife Jessica and I have overcome.

I grew up in Squamish, BC, where, as a small boy, I gained a true appreciation for the steep forested hills and ocean that surrounds it. When I was 20, I got a job working for my stepfather prospecting for gold. That's where I met my beautiful, outgoing wife, in St. Stephen, NB, where the East Coast meets the West Coast. I tell people, "I was looking for gold, but I found a diamond."

Soon after we met and she was persuaded to join me, we moved to Abbotsford, BC. There I rented a 150′ barn and filled it to the brim with everything from driftwood to free firewood. I would salvage an entire log, literally dragging it down the road with my 10′ trailer, milling everything with my Alaskan mill. It was a struggle, but was satisfying when I learned how to combine carpentry with my previous knowledge of logging.

After partly prefabbing the house in the barn, I was led to the perfect foundation: a small 68′ × 30′ retired inter-island BC ferry with an 18′ ramp and a small crane. It was perfect for the build, but came with many challenges when I pulled the little barge up the Fraser River to start construction.

Once I arrived up the river in Mission, BC, I was greeted by some locals who had opinions about what I should be doing. Keeping freedom in mind, I was off like a bird from the fowler's nest, headed back home as soon as the basic structure was complete.

First I had to overcome what I heard someone call "the storm of the century" in the Howe Sound, which almost led to my being shipwrecked in the middle of the night. But daybreak came and I literally entered the Cattermole Slough in Squamish through a rainbow at the entrance.

Squamish is the port town of Whistler, and we arrived just in time for the 2010 Winter Olympics. Although we've had only positive feedback from locals, as well from travelers who visit Squamish just to see the houseboat they call Noah's Ark, it's been a battle to try to establish a sustainable houseboat community.

Our boat is well on its way to being completely self-contained, with everything from composting toilets to rain catchment and saltwater desalination system. It's far from finished, but it's almost time to move in.

When I was starting, someone said that if I knew how much work it would be, I probably wouldn't have started it. Who knows?

I'm glad I was able to take the project one step at a time. I never become overwhelmed because of good family support.

For more details on this houseboat and other recent construction, you can contact me at the website below; I would love feedback.

www.MeilingerWoodDesign.com

> *"First I had to overcome what I heard someone call 'the storm of the century' in the Howe Sound, which almost led to my being shipwrecked in the middle of the night."*

"I'm glad I was able to take the project one step at a time. I never become overwhelmed because of good family support."

Dianne's Rose

Roy Schreyer

Dianne's Rose is a small, "tiny" if you will, house/shanty/camp boat that my wife inspired me to design. She never liked the "tippy" side of sailing and one day commented she'd come out more if we had a comfortable boat.

This 17′ × 8′ beam, houseboat is the result. Needing only 6″ to float, it is perfect for sneaking into shallow coves and pulling up to isolated beaches — a feature we enjoyed in our sailboat. A refined barge hull was the solution needed to achieve this draft and the accommodations for Dianne's comfort.

A kitchenette is on the opposite side, with a propane cook top. The space under the rear deck is utilized as a pantry and cooler for food storage.

Hang a privacy curtain across the aisle, and the back of the boat becomes a full bathroom. Toilet, sink, and bathing. Set up camp style of course, using a basin to stand in and pitcher to wet and rinse. Hot water provided from a heated pot or solar bag!

The front, 4′ × 8′, and back, 28″ × 8′, decks add to the livability of the small cabin. Storage is below and porches outside.

The front porch could be tented in to provide additional sleeping space similar to

> "The boat has had some unforeseen uses at home on its trailer (saving marina costs), as a 'man cave,' guest house, and second bathroom."

The cabin, 8′ × 10′, has areas that perform dual function (or more). There are two couches, 62″ long, facing each other, that serve as lounge, driver's seat, dining and sleeping areas.

We have a queen-sized bed when filler boards are in place! These boards morph into the dining table and additional seats and then again into the steps and storage shelves under the decks.

There is a small bathroom on the left rear side, 32″ × 36″, with full standing headroom.

The composting toilet (which does not smell) can slide under the rear deck to create a private changing room.

"pop-up" tent trailers. This could make a small family comfortable on extended outings!

The boat has had some unforeseen uses at home on its trailer (saving marina costs), as a "man cave," guest house, and second bathroom. (We live in Wasaga Beach, Ontario, Canada.)

Dianne's Rose was launched June 15th, 2013, so we'll get to know her better, but she is already making us very happy. The small size is a large part of the fun!

Our motor is small as well, a 9.8 hp outboard. Fuel costs are not a worry and will not interfere with our enjoyment of the beautiful scenery as it passes by at a steady 6 mph (¾ throttle).

> "There are two couches, 62″ long, facing each other, that serve as lounge, driver's seat, dining and sleeping areas."

> "A kitchenette on the opposite side with the same-sized counter, having a propane cook top and sink, utilizes space under the rear deck as a pantry and cooler storage..."

"Needing only 6″ to float, it is perfect for sneaking into shallow coves and pulling up to isolated beaches."

The Moron Brothers of Kentucky & Their Shantyboat

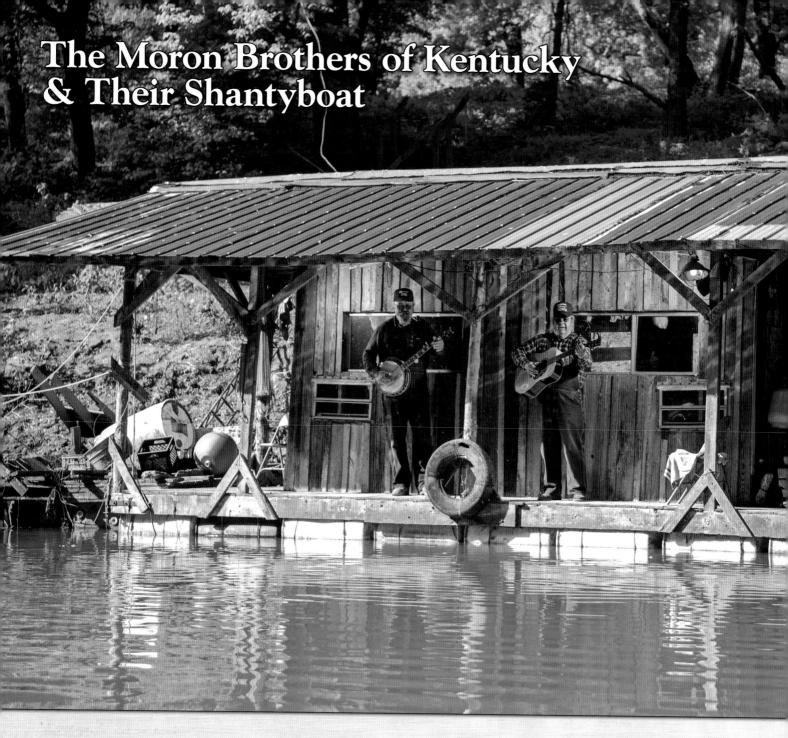

"It's a little tin tarpaper shack, built on the water..."

About a year ago I ran across the YouTube video (**www.shltr.net/mikemike**) of the Moron Brothers, which had been viewed over a million times. It was totally charming; these guys were relaxed and funny, and their floating boys' club with wood stove and kerosene lanterns came across as comfortable and fun.

We tried to contact them, but no luck for about a year. Then in February 2013, I got hold of Mike Carr (Lardo), who said he lives on a hill above the Kentucky River, with the shantyboat parked on the bank down the hill. They push (not tow) the houseboat with a 20′ flat-bottom Jon boat and a 50 hp

Honda outboard. Mike's partner is Mike Hammond (Burley).

Mike said he'd been a little reluctant to talk to someone from California, because he is a trapper. I told Mike I'd considered being a taxidermist when I was a kid, and now picked up road kill for food and fur. Well, that got him, and he said, "Anyone who eats road kill is on the same page as me!"

He also says they just got a good internet hookup and are "high-tech rednecks."

The Morons are actually a bluegrass duo. I was surprised how good they are — I got three CDs from their website.(I recommend listening to "River Rats" while you

read this.) They tour with their wives, and don't fly.

Here are the boys talking in the video:

MY DADDY RAISED me on the water, raised me in the woods. Other than pickin' the banjo, I guess if I had my choice, I'd lay around on the river.

It's a little tin tarpaper shack, built on the water...yessir, there ain't been no Beverly Hillbillies have a home on the water...

Lardo: We're actually twins. I know it's hard to believe, but when Daddy seen us laying

"My daddy raised me on the water, raised me in the woods."

Photos by Tim Webb

"Man, I tell ya, ... makes me feel like a kid again."

there for the first time, we were little baby boys, he told Mama you have to drown that ugly one. That's how come he learned to swim before I did,

Burley: Learning to swim wasn't too tough, but getting outta that burlap bag was a trick *(laughter).* Them concrete blocks was heavy....

We play for fun, mostly. If we wanted to own our own house, we'd get into something else, but bluegrass, there ain't no money in it much.... We play around at all the major festivals in Kentucky, and we got three albums out....

Somethin' about the smell of coffee perkin', and coal oil

lamps burnin' just reminds me of when I was a kid and I could come down here and turn the radio on and light a coal oil lamp and build a fire in the stove and listen to the Grand Ole Opry on a Saturday night...Man, I tell ya, it's pretty nice, makes me feel like a kid again.

Got beans and peppers, got popcorn, sugar, beets. We had some government cheese but we ate it all *(laughter)*...You know you're a redneck when you slice the 'maters and onions and baloney up with the same knife as you field-dressed a deer...

If we'd a-had baloney during the Civil War, we'd a won *(laughter).*

More

"We got it made, don't we, come down here and float down the river and fish and hunt and sleep..."

On building the houseboat:

"I guess all in all it took me two to three months. I told Burley when I got it done, I said look at it, she's all mine, handmade... he says it looks like you made it with your feet to me *(laughter)*... two beds, a table, a wood stove.

Living on the river, we come down here and get off in this little shantyboat, I don't know, it just frees your mind up and there's not a whole lot to do except write songs and look at nature....

We got it made, don't we, come down here and float down the river and fish and hunt and sleep.... That's what a ̶d government job would do ̶..."

That's basically about it, two beds, a table, a wood stove, and it's mobile, we can take her up and down the river when we want to...."

How did you get the name "Moron Brothers?"

"...Our first job together. When we come off stage and went to our seats with our wives to watch the next act, the guy next to my wife asked her if she saw those two morons that was up there a minute ago, meaning us. That is when the Moron Brothers was born.

His name was Mike and my name was Mike, so Lardo and Burley was invented to separate the two Mikes.

We both are fortunate to come from strong, hard-working, religious families from the heart of bluegrass country.

Our wives travel with us and sell tapes, CDs, and T-shirts. Without their support and work,

we couldn't and wouldn't do it. Mainly because we're still mostly doing it for fun...."

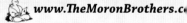 *www.TheMoronBrothers.c*

"...we're still mostly doing it for fun."

La Fille— Tugboat Home

Drew and Deb McVittie

DREW AND DEB McVITTIE and their three excited kids, Kathryn, Bryan and Jaimie, became the proud owners of a steel tug named The Seaspan Tempest in November, 1998. The rust didn't deter Drew from seeing the possibilities for this 35-year-old vessel, and he soon had family and friends scraping and painting her bottom and getting her ready to cruise the West Coast of British Columbia.

The first thing the family did was to restore the tug's original name, La Fille. Major structural changes included removing the towing engine and replacing it with one that is smaller and more fuel efficient; fabricating a ̀ain cabin to extend the short ̀lhouse by 18 feet; moving the engine room bulkhead back to create a double cabin; adding two heads and a roughed-in galley; creating an airy bunk room; and building a set of curved stairs between the upper and lower decks.

The main cabin and bunk rooms weren't built until the second year the McVittie's had the tug, so the first year they dropped their old tent trailer on the back deck and headed out with five kids for a spring break holiday. Apart from the fact that the ice in the coolers melted in about four hours on the steel deck, and Deb and Drew had to sleep on the wheelhouse floor (the kids got the tent trailer), they had a fantastic trip. Passing boats inevitably did a double-take when they realized

just what was passing them by on the water.

La Fille is still a work in progress (aren't all boats!), but a big electric stove, a "real" fridge, flushing toilets, and a shower make her comfy for coastal cruising year round. The areas that are completed have local yellow cedar, fir, and cherry wood paneling. She has hosted friends and family, young and old (including a wedding on Bowen Island), writers from around the world (at the Vancouver International Writers Festival over the past few years), book clubs and stitch & bitch clubs, scuba divers and the Blackberry Boys. The kayaks and rowboat are strapped to the roof, the BBQ is tucked under stern bulwarks, the

"Passing boats inevitably did a double-take . . ."

fridge and freezer are stocked, the bookshelf is full, the dogs are happy, and the West Coast is one of the most fascinating places on earth. What more could a person ask for?

Vital Statistics

Length: 58´
Beam: 20´
Draft: 9´

Weight: 85 tons

Main engine: Cummins 855 (340 hp @ 1800 rpm)

Gensets: Kabota 12.5 kW and Detroit Diesel 30 kW

Inverter: 2000 watts

"The rust didn't deter Drew from seeing the possibilities . . ."

"La Fille is still a work in progress (aren't all boats!) . . ."

*Right: La Fille when
we first got her*

209

Bibliography

SOME OF THESE BOOKS ARE NOT CURRENTLY IN print, but we have included them since it is not that difficult to track down out-of-print books these days online. **Note:** abebooks.com often has lower prices than Amazon.

Airstreams: Custom Interiors
David Winick
Schiffer Publishing (2010)
ISBN: 978-0-764335-39-6
David Winnick restores vintage Airstream trailers and in this book shows his meticulous interior design work.

An Island to Oneself
Tom Neale
Ox Bow Press (1990)
ISBN: 978-0-918024-76-3
The story of bush craft and survival enthusiast Tom Neale living alone on a small coral atoll near the Cook Islands for six years.

Around the World Single-Handed
Harry Pidgeon
Dover Publications (1989)
ISBN: 978-0-486259-46-8
Harry Pidgeon circumnavigated the globe in the early 1900s in his 34-foot homemade yawl, and wrote a classic adventure book, including encounters with native peoples, navigating through raging storms, and running aground off the coast of South Africa. 60 black and white photos.

The Complete Book of Boondock RVing
Bill and Jan Moeller
International Marine/Ragged Mountain Press (2007)
ISBN: 978-0-071490-65-8
If you are tired of being crammed into spaces at RV parks and want a little more space, this is your complete guide to camping without hookups.

The Brendan Voyage
Tim Severin
Modern Library (2000)
ISBN: 978-0-375755-24-8
Tim Severin's voyage from Ireland to Newfoundland in a boat modeled on a 6th century leather boat (*a curragh*), retracing the journeys of both mythical and historic figures.

Tiny Homes on the Move Blogs and Websites

Here are some websites for nomadic homes. If you know of other good ones, please advise, and we'll add them in subsequent printings.:
- www.CanalScape.net
- www.CheapRVLiving.com
- www.CruisersForum.com
- www.NomadicHome.com
- www.ShantyboatLiving.com
- www.Skoolie.net
- www.TravellerHomes.co.uk
- www.TruckCamperPorn.com
- www.VanDwellers.org

Dirt-Cheap Survival Retreat
M.D Creekmore
Paladin Press (2011)
ISBN: 978-1-581607-47-5
A guide to finding suitable land, buying a used trailer, growing and storing food, providing alternative power sources, and living off the grid.

Dreams on Wheels: Modern Do-It-Yourself Gypsies
Ben Rosander
RV-Busconversions.com (2004)
ISBN: 978-0-972470-43-8
A homemade-looking book on twenty or so buses converted to homes, shops, and food trucks. 200 photos, drawings, and floor plans. Hit the road, Jack!

Freewheeling Homes
David Pearson
Chelsea Green (2002)
ISBN: 978-1-931498-03-6
An array of custom-built homes on wheels as well as explanations of how you can build your own and make your dreams a reality.

Houseboats: Aquatic Architecture of Sausalito
Kathy Schaffer
Schiffer Publishing (2007)
ISBN: 978-0-764327-22-3
There are lots of books on houseboats, but this is about the best. Tons of color photos of the famed houseboat community of Sausalito, California.

In The Heart of the Sea: The Tragedy of the Whaleship Essex
Nathaniel Philbrick
Penguin Books (2001)
ISBN: 978-0-141001-82-1
The gripping story of the whaleship Essex, which set sail in 1819 from Nantucket for the South Pacific, where it was rammed and sunk by an angry sperm whale. The crew drifted for more than ninety days on three small whaleboats, eventually resorting to cannibalism to stay alive. Three men survived.

Life Nomadic
Tynan
Create Space Independent Publishing Platform (2010)
ISBN: 978-1-449536-62-6
Learn how to travel on the cheap: Cruises for $30 a day, flights for as little as $20, and cheap hotel stays.

Living High
June Burn
Griffin Bay Book Store (1992)
ISBN: 978-0-963456-20-5
The Burn family's glorious adventures home-steading in the Pacific Northwest, teaching Eskimos near Siberia, and exploring the United States in a homemade 1922 Dodge house car.

Manifold Destiny: The One! The Only! Guide to Cooking on Your Car Engine
Chris Maynard and Bill Scheller
Simon & Schuster (2008)
ISBN: 978-1-416596-23-3
Cook chicken and fish on your car engine while traveling using aluminum foil. Dozens of recipes, including Cajun shrimp, red-flannel hash, and leg of lamb. Why not?

Mobile Saunas
Karlis Otto Kalnins
Lulu.com (2012)
ISBN: 978-1-105258-65-7
Sauna trucks, sauna buses, sauna trailers, sauna boats, trail sweats, great ideas on mobile saunas. Lots of good color photos.

My Cool Campervan: An Inspirational Guide to Retro-Style Campervans
Jane Field-Lewis and Chris Haddon
Pavilion (2010)
ISBN: 978-1-862059-05-4

Highly recommended book from the UK, of vintage campervans, with great photos of unique vehicles.

My Cool Caravan: An Inspirational Guide to Retro-Style Caravans
Jane Field-Lewis and Chris Haddon
Pavilion (2010)
ISBN: 978-1-862058-78-1

Another great book, this one of old small trailers, mostly European, that are charming, idiosyncratic and/or unusual, and that are aesthetically pleasing homes for the road.

Overland Journal
Published 5 times annually
www.overlandjournal.com

A classy magazine by two guys interested in vehicle-supported expedition travel but dissatisfied with the paradigm of 4WD and adventure motorcycle magazines — which stress conquering the wilderness rather than exploring the world.

Rolling Shelter: Vehicles We Have Called Home
Kelly Hart
Hartworks, Inc. (2013)
ISBN: 978-0-916289-37-9

This is a personal account of Kelly and Rosanna Hart's life in two different buses, three vans, two small motor homes, two travel trailers combined into one house, and two cars. This book will inspire you and give you ideas on using vehicles as homes. The book contains 200 photographs and five detailed floor plans, with descriptions of the conversions, as well as stories of the Hart's adventures in the U.S., Mexico, and Guatemala.

Sailing Back in Time: A Nostalgic Voyage on Canada's West Coast
Maria Coffey
Whitecap Books (2010)
ISBN: 978-1-552853-38-2

Maria Coffey and Dag Goering's tale of a three-month journey by way of wooden boat along Canada's West Coast. The couple sailed in tandem with Allen and Sharie Farrell, who were aboard their exquisite junk-rigged China Cloud.

Sea Quest: Global Blue Water Adventuring
Charles A. Borden (1979)
David McKay Company
ISBN: 978-0-679513-57-5

A well-written account of global sailing in all sorts of boats past, present, and future.

Silver Palaces
Douglas Keister
Gibbs Smith (2004)
ISBN: 978-1-586853-52-5

Vintage trailer expert Douglas Keister takes you through the inception and evolution of the streamlined aluminum trailer.

Sisters on the Fly
Irene Rawlings
Andrews McMeel Publishing (2010)
ISBN: 978-0-740791-31-4

An all-girl group (3,000+) who buy and restore vintage trailers, then camp out together all over the USA — fly-fishing, exploring, swimming, cooking, singing, dancing, and hanging out.

Small Ships — Working Vessels and Workboat Heritage Yacht Designs
Jay Benford
Tiller Publishing (2002)
ISBN: 978-1-888671-41-4

A book of plans for living aboard tugboats, ferries, trawler yachts, houseboats, and fishing vessels. Each plan has the boat's history as well as photos. "Every one is a salty and practical cruising vessel...."

Some Turtles Have Nice Shells
Roger D. Beck
Pine Hill Graphics (2002)
ISBN: 978-0-971410-36-7

A classic by now (out of print), with a wealth of information from Roger D. Beck about house trucks and house buses.

Teardrops and Tiny Trailers
Douglas Keister
Gibbs Smitgh (2008)
ISBN: 978-1-423602-74-3

The definitive book on diminutive vintage teardrop trailers and "canned ham" trailers, with spiffy color photos.

The Voyage of the Cormorant
Christian Beamish
Patagonia Books (2012)
ISBN: 978-0-980122-76-3

Christian Beamish, a former associate editor at *Surfers Journal*, built an 18-foot open style Scandinavian sailboat in his garage and sailed and surfed the coast of Baja California, using line-of-sight navigation and a GPS (and a 9´ 6˝ long board).

Voyages of a Simple Sailor
Roger D. Taylor
The Fitzroy Press (2008)
ISBN: 978-0-955803-50-5

At 23, Roger Taylor got a job on the square-rigger Endeavour II, bound for New Zealand. The boat crashed on rocks in the darkness of night in a tropical storm. Taylor managed to survive the crash and went on to build his own boat and twice crossed the Tasman Sea. From these experiences he developed his ideas on simplicity in ocean voyaging.

Credits

Editor & Layout: Lloyd Kahn
Book Builder: Rick Gordon
Associate Editor & Layout: Lew Lewandowski*
Contributing Editor: Evan Kahn
Art Director: David Wills
Proofreaders: Robert Grenier & Susan Friedland
Office Manager: Mary Sangster

*Lew, in his web perambulations, came up with a lot of these homes.

With a Lot of Help from Our Friends:

- Justin Anthony
- Tod Beeson
- Bill Bullis
- Lesley Creed
- Kirsten Dirksen
- Google Alerts
- Kent Griswold
- Sean Hellfritsch
- Kim Herter
- Richard Jones
- Andy Lee
- Greg Marcotte
- Trevor Perlman
- Prepress and Press Crew at Paramount Printing
- Publishers Group West Crew
- Tilikum Redding
- Bill Lam
- Trevor Shih
- Godfrey Stephens
- Mike W
- Kai Watkins
- Alan Whittle
- www.faircompanies.com
- www.23breaths.com
- www.tinyhouseblog.com
- www.tinyhousenews.info

Note: We've tried to keep track of anyone that helped in any way; if we've missed anyone (emailing, phoning, telling us about one of these homes), please let us know and we'll add your name to the above list.

Photos: There are over 1,100 photos here, all from different contributors. Rick Gordon spent over a month upgrading and improving the files. In some cases we've had to make do with less-than-desirable photo files: content trumping style. We wish everything could be crystal-clear, with rich colors, but in a few cases, we've had to use smartphone or otherwise low-resolution photos — all that was available.

Production Hardware: Macintosh computers (Mac Pro and MacBook Pro), NEC professional graphics monitors, Epson Stylus Pro 4800 printer, Microtek and Nikon scanners

Production Software: Adobe InDesign, Adobe Photoshop, Adobe Acrobat Pro, Microsoft Word, AppleScript Editor, SilverFast and Vuescan scanning software

Printing: Paramount/Book Art, Inc., Hong Kong
Press: Mitsubishi 3000 LS4
Paper: Text: 128gsm Matt Art
         Cover: 250gsm C1S Art Card

Production Process: A detailed description of our old-school (to begin with) production process is on the last page of *Tiny Homes,* and it's basically the same here: we accumulate information for a year or more, then start doing layout two pages at a time.

We use an inexpensive color copy machine to scale photos to size, and then tape them down to the layout sheets along with the text. Next, David fine-tunes them, again by hand, before they are passed along to Rick, who then begins the digital process. Eventually the entire book is transmitted via FTP (on the internet) to our printers in Hong Kong.

The proofing process then begins, and once we approve of everything, the printers make the plates used on the presses directly from the digital files; this is called DTP, or "direct to plate."

I'll be going to Hong Kong this spring to oversee the printing. I do this with each of our color books for the first printing. Not many publishers do it these days, but I want to be there to make sure the colors are right; plus I love printing plants — the hustle, the press action, the smell of ink, the camaraderie with press men.

It might take a day and a half to print the entire book, and I'll show up every 2–3 hours for the next 16-page signature. With *Tiny Homes,* I spent one night in a small room at the plant, and would get a phone call wakeup for each new signature.

I think being there and working with the press guys gives the book a little something extra, a little better quality. And once you get it right the first time, they have it dialed in for all subsequent printings. (*Tiny Homes* just had its 7th printing.)

—LK

Left to right: Lew, David, Rick, Lloyd, Evan

TheShelterBlog.com
This book is ongoing!

OVER THE PAST FEW YEARS, AND WITH INCREASING frequency, we're hearing from people who were influenced to build a house, or to change their lives, due to reading one of our books. It's been not only surprising, but gratifying, something I could never have foreseen.

A couple of things have happened here:

1. We're developing an ever-stronger network of self-reliant people who want to communicate what they're discovering.

2. We have a huge backup, growing daily, of good material. Things are pouring in. Stories, photos, leads. We have some 1,600 photos in our files for sequels to *Home Work*, *Tiny Homes*, and *Tiny Homes on the Move*.

What to do with it all? Right now we file it away for future books, but it takes a long time before any of it appears in print.

The answer: *TheShelterBlog.com,* with the focus on shelter and related subjects: small homes, tiny homes, homesteading, design, fixer-uppers, building materials, carpentry, crafts, tools and tips, gardening, foraging, fishing, etc.

I have my own blog, but it's highly eclectic. It includes shelter material, but also music, skateboarding, animals, computers, media, surfing, anything interesting I run across. Our new blog, by contrast, will stick to the subject of shelter.

We have something unique here. We're not just fishing around on the Internet, as is so commonly done these days. We're generating our own content: these people and stories are coming directly to us. Most of it is brand new, and there's a chain of continuity. No other website or blog has this focus or a network like this.

It feels a bit now like it did 40+ years ago when we were station-central on handmade housing for like-minded people. We got tons of input, and *Shelter* (1973) was the result.

Now, we seem to be in another vortex. We've become headquarters of sorts for people interested in handmade, homemade shelter, and artistic, colorful, lively homes.

The difference now is that we have the Internet to expand our communications. Now we can communicate instantly, rather than accumulating large files of photos and stories for some future book.

The blog is the other arm of our communications on shelter and building: real hold-in-your-hands books — one every 2–3 years, paired with digital transmission of shelter news daily. We invite you to send us your information — at **www.TheShelterBlog.com**.

Architecture Book of the Year

Builders of the Pacific Coast
by Lloyd Kahn

$28.95
9″ × 12″
256 pages, 1,200 images
ISBN: 978-0-936070-43-8

A UNIQUE STYLE OF CARPENTRY has developed over the past 40 years along the west coast of North America. This book, three years in the making, features photos and interviews with builders from San Francisco up the coast to Vancouver Island, BC. From unique homesteads on the California coast, to communities of owner-built shelters on small islands in the Strait of Georgia, to tuned-in beachfront houses on the "Wild Coast" of Vancouver Island, these structures are creative and unique.

There are three featured builders: Lloyd House, master craftsman and designer who has created a series of unique homes on a small island; Bruce Atkey, builder of a number of houses and lodges built of hand-split cedar on the Wild Coast; and SunRay Kelley, barefoot builder in tune with nature, who has designed and built wildly imaginative structures in Washington and California. In addition, there are sculptural buildings

of driftwood, homes that are beautiful as well as practical, live-aboard boats, and stunning architectural design.

"On every page is something shocking and delightful. A boat with legs. A roof like a leaf. A caravan with eyes. A split-cedar woodshed shaped like a bird. Stair rails so sinuous and snakey they might come to life and grab you. Sculpted earth walls. Round windows and arched doors. Roofs curved like seagull wings...."

–Mike Litchfield, *West Marin Citizen*

"...an exhilarating look at the North Coast. Inspiring! An exciting immersion..."

–Jim Macey, Keeler, Calif.

The Sequel to *Shelter*

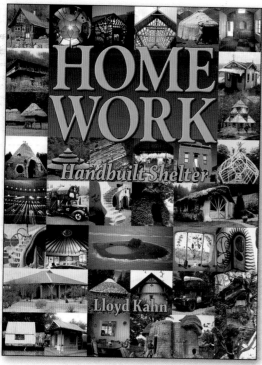

Home Work
Handbuilt Shelter
by Lloyd Kahn

$28.95
9″ × 12″
256 pages
ISBN: 978-0-936070-33-9

50,000 COPIES IN PRINT

H OME WORK IS LLOYD KAHN'S sequel to *Shelter* and illustrates new and even more imaginative ways to put a roof over your head, some of which were inspired by *Shelter* itself. *Home Work* showcases the ultimate in human ingenuity, building construction, and ecocentric lifestyle. What *Shelter* was to '60s counterculture, *Home Work* is to the "green building revolution," and more.

Home Work describes homes built from the soul, inventiveness free from social constraint, but created with a solid understanding of natural materials, structure, and aesthetics. From yurts to caves to tree houses to tents, thatched houses, glass houses, nomadic homes, and riverboats, each handbuilt dwelling finds itself at one with its environment, using natural materials.

Home Work features over 1,000 photos and 300 line drawings. Here are stories of real people building and living in their

own houses, plus Kahn's observations gathered over the 30 years since *Shelter* was first published.

"The book is delicious, soulful, elating, inspiring, courageous, compassionate..."

–Peter Nabokov, Chair, Dept. of World Arts and Cultures, UCLA

"*Home Work* is a KNOCKOUT."

–John van der Zee, author of *Agony in the Garden*

"...a kaleidoscopic portrait of human ingenuity"

–San Francisco Chronicle

"...we can't stop looking at it!!"

Scaling Back in the 21st Century

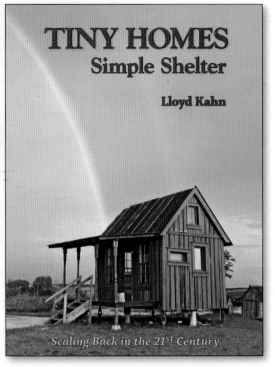

Tiny Homes
Simple Shelter
by Lloyd Kahn

$28.95
9″ × 12″
224 pages, 1,300 images
ISBN: 978-0-936070-52-0

"…A glorious portfolio…"
   –Penelope Green, *New York Times*

"…A genuine hit…"
   –Jeffrey Trachtenberg,
   Wall Street Journal

"Gives me chills, it's so inspiring."
   –Cheryl Long, Editor,
   The Mother Earth News

"A '…photo-packed new volume…(by) Shelter Publications founder and green architecture pioneer Lloyd Kahn…'"
   –*Publishers Weekly*

"…a cornucopia of 1,300 photos…Tiny though they are, they are much more than mere shelter."
   –Kevin Kelly, kk.org/cooltools

T HERE'S A GRASSROOTS MOVEMENT IN tiny homes these days. The real estate collapse, the economic downturn, people burning out on 12-hour workdays—many people are rethinking their ideas about shelter—seeking an alternative to high rents, or a lifelong mortgage debt to a bank on an overpriced home.

In this book are some 150 builders who have taken things into their own hands, creating tiny homes (under 500 sq. ft.). Homes on land, homes on wheels, homes on the road, homes on water, even homes in the trees. There are also studios, saunas, garden sheds, and greenhouses.

There are 1,300 photos, showing a rich variety of small homemade shelters, and there are stories (and thoughts and inspirations) of the owner-builders who are on the forefront of this new trend in downsizing and self-sufficiency.

Many people have decided to scale back, to get by with less stuff, to live in smaller homes. You can buy a ready-made tiny home, build your own, get a kit or prefab, or live in a bus, houseboat, or other movable shelter. Some cities have special ordinances for building "inlaw" or "granny flats" in the backyard. There are innovative solutions in cities, such as the "capsules" in Tokyo. There are numerous blogs and websites with news, photos, and/or plans for tiny homes, documented here.

If you're thinking of scaling back, you'll find plenty of inspiration here. Here's a different approach, a 180° turn from increasing consumption. Here are builders, designers, architects (no less), dreamers, artists, road gypsies, and water dwellers who've achieved a measure of freedom and independence by taking shelter into their own hands.

Our 1973 Classic on Building

Shelter
Edited by Lloyd Kahn

$28.95
11″ × 14½″
176 pages
ISBN: 978-0-936070-11-7

"How very fine it is to leaf through a 176-page book on architecture — and find no palaces, no pyramids or temples, no cathedrals, skyscrapers, Kremlins or Pentagons in sight … instead, a book of homes, habitations for human beings in all their infinite variety."
   –Edward Abbey,
   Natural History magazine

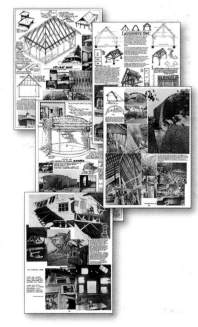

W ITH OVER 1,000 photographs, *Shelter* is a classic celebrating the imagination, resourcefulness, and exuberance of human habitat. First published in 1973, it is not only a record of the counter-cultural builders of the '60s, but also of buildings all over the world. It includes a history of shelter and the evolution of building types: tents, yurts, timber buildings, barns, small homes, domes, etc. There is a section on building materials, including heavy timber construction and stud framing, as well as stone, straw bale construction, adobe, plaster, and bamboo. There are interviews with builders and tips on recycled materials and wrecking. The emphasis is on creating your own shelter (or space) with your own hands. A joyful, inspiring book.

Hobo Buddha

IN NOVEMBER 1972, MY FRIEND JACK FULTON and I took off on a road trip to New Mexico to shoot photos for our forthcoming book *Shelter*. It was a rich trip. In fact, it was a rich time in America for a bunch of us who wanted to do things for ourselves — like building our own homes. The *Whole Earth Catalog* had connected a lot of like-minded people, and our subject in this counter-cultural kaleidoscope was building — shelter.

On the trip we shot photos and interviewed builders in New Mexico and Colorado. On the way home, we dropped down to Highway 50, known as "The Loneliest Highway in America."

It was a cold, bright, sunshiny day; snow on the sagebrush. No other cars. Just a little west of Austin, we saw a lone figure in the distance, passed him, and turned back and met Armand Bassett.

Armand said he'd been walking about 10 years, ate out of roadside trash cans, didn't accept rides, and figured he'd walked the equivalent of six times around the world. He was carrying all his stuff in a Purina Chow dog food bag.

Here we were working on a book on shelter and this man had survived without any shelter for a decade. As we got ready to take off, we gave Armand some peanut butter. I said to him, "Look at us, in a car, warm, with sleeping bags, food, money, and all you've got is in that bag."

He looked straight at me and said: "It's all the same. You're on the road, I'm on the road…"

— • • —

For some reason, as we were finishing this book on nomadic shelter, this image of Armand flashed before my eyes. It seems as if his spirit has resurfaced here, some 40 years later.